LEARN YOUR GUITAR SCALES

Tips & Techniques

MODES, PENTATONICS & ARPEGGIOS EXPLAINED

LUKE ZECCHIN

Getting lost on the guitar neck?
Finally, fretboard memorization made easy!

If you like this book, you'll love our **Fretboard Memorization Workshop**! This online master class is your shortcut to demystifying the fretboard puzzle. Here you'll be guided step-by-step through the key concepts, techniques, and exercises needed to master your entire fretboard–quickly and easily. These insights have helped thousands of students worldwide, and we're certain they'll help you too!

For more information, head to **LearnYourFretboard.com**.

This book is dedicated to my wonderful parents. Thank you for buying my first guitar, coming to my gigs, and never telling me to get a real job.

Copyright © 2019 Luke Zecchin

ISBN: 978-0-9925507-8-3

All rights reserved. No part of this publication may be reproduced in any form or by any means without express written consent from the author.

Published by **GuitarIQ.com**

Copyedited by Allister Thompson

Proofread by Dan Foster

Illustrated by Jasmin Zecchin

The author and publisher have made every effort to ensure the information contained in this book is both relevant and accurate at the time of release. They accept no responsibility for any loss, injury, or inconvenience sustained by any person using this book or the information provided within it.

Contents

Online Bonus Material 7

Preface 9

Introduction 11

1 | Foundational Concepts 13
    Why Scales? 14
    Understanding Scales 15
    Using Scales 17
    Learning Scales 19

2 | Octave Shapes 21
    Using Octave Shapes 22
    Octave Shapes 24

3 | Modes 25
    Understanding Modes 26
    Using Modes 29
    Playing Modes 32
    The Ionian Mode 34
    The Dorian Mode 35
    The Phrygian Mode 36
    The Lydian Mode 37
    The Mixolydian Mode 38
    The Aeolian Mode 39
    The Locrian Mode 40
    Exercise 1 41
    Exercise 2 42

4 | Pentatonic Scales ... 43

- Understanding Pentatonic Scales ... 44
- Using Pentatonic Scales ... 46
- Playing Pentatonic Scales ... 49
- Major Pentatonic Scales ... 51
- Major Blues Scales ... 52
- Minor Pentatonic Scales ... 53
- Minor Blues Scales ... 54
- Exercise 3 ... 55
- Exercise 4 ... 56

5 | Arpeggios ... 57

- Understanding Arpeggios ... 58
- Using Arpeggios ... 60
- Playing Arpeggios ... 63
- Major Arpeggios ... 65
- Minor Arpeggios ... 66
- Major Seventh Arpeggios ... 67
- Minor Seventh Arpeggios ... 68
- Dominant Seventh Arpeggios ... 69
- Minor Seven Flat Five Arpeggios ... 70
- Exercise 5 ... 71
- Exercise 6 ... 72

6 | Scales in Context ... 73

- Thinking in Context ... 74
- Playing in Context ... 76
- Practicing in Context ... 77

Final Thoughts 81

Liked This Book? 82

Additional Resources 83

About the Author 84

Get Your Free Online Bonus Now!

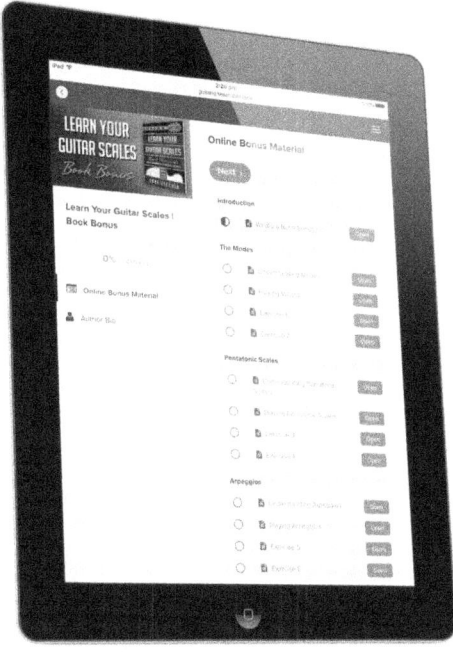

This book comes complete with free online bonus material. We've compiled a companion website to enhance your reading experience. Extras include audio examples, backing tracks, bonus downloads, and more!

Get your free bonus content at: **www.guitariq.com/lygs-bonus**

Preface

Welcome, and thank you for choosing **Learn Your Guitar Scales**.

For many guitar players, learning scales can quickly become overwhelming. In part, this is due to the seemingly endless scale types and alternatives that exist. It can be complex enough memorizing the names of all these scales, let alone what they look like on the fretboard and how to use them! While feeling intimidated is understandable, it isn't necessary. There are numerous languages in the world, but a person doesn't need to know them all to say something worthwhile.

The intention of this book is to focus on the central elements that will have the greatest impact on your playing. These foundational concepts and patterns will enable you to navigate a broad range of playing situations, regardless of style or genre. Mastering the fundamentals is infinitely more beneficial than being overwhelmed by so many options that you end up using none of them effectively.

This highlights a common frustration with many scale books for guitar. Being shown a multitude of scale patterns on the fretboard can be useful, but it provides little explanation regarding how to actually learn, practice, and apply them. What's the point of knowing all this information if we can't make something musical out of it?

In contrast, the focus here isn't simply on demonstrating what different patterns *look* like, but on explaining how they're built, how they relate to one another, and how they're commonly used. Touching on everything from basic concepts to more advanced applications, we'll take a detailed look at the formative scales and arpeggios that shape the essential creative framework for guitar.

I sincerely hope this book provides renewed insight and inspires continued development and innovation in your playing.

—Luke Zecchin

Introduction

In light of the vast amount of existing material on guitar scales, it seems appropriate to start by outlining what this book is *not*. This isn't intended to be a collection of every possible guitar scale you might encounter. While a scale *encyclopedia* like that might occasionally be a helpful reference, in reality a resource of such magnitude is likely to confuse as many guitar players as it helps. More importantly, it's very unlikely most of that information would contribute to your core musical vocabulary on guitar.

Instead, this guide focuses on patterns rooted in the *diatonic* world, or in other words, scales and arpeggios that are derived from the same key center. Why? These diatonic patterns underpin the foundations of all Western music. As such, an extremely wide range of musical situations, spanning numerous genres, can be successfully navigated using just these core patterns.

The concepts and patterns discussed in this book will form an extensive creative framework for crafting your musical ideas. The goal is to narrow our focus to the vital elements that provide the most creative options. Not only will this give you the biggest return for your effort, but it will also provide the necessary foundations should you later experiment with broader concepts.

In this book, we'll take an in-depth look at fundamental patterns such as octave shapes, the major scale and all its modes, pentatonic scales, blues scales, and various arpeggios (including major seventh, minor seventh, dominant seventh, and more). In addition to outlining and explaining each of these patterns, we'll explore their numerous positions and alternate shapes across the fretboard. We'll also discuss foundational ideas for understanding scales, common uses for each pattern covered, key exercises and techniques for effective learning, and central concepts for using these scales and arpeggios in context.

Each pattern covered in this guide is *movable*, so rather than redundantly outlining every shape in various keys, all scales and arpeggios will be demonstrated from the same starting position, or *root* note, across the fretboard. This has the added benefit of displaying how these patterns are similar and distinct from one another in context.

Lastly, since some concepts introduced may initially feel foreign or difficult, it's important to be conscious of playing fatigue. Be sure to practice at comfortable tempos, and don't forget to take regular breaks when playing. We're going to cover a lot of content, so it's important to work through this book at your own pace. While this information has been streamlined to be easily digestible, the learning process will be different for each person.

1

Foundational Concepts

Before looking at any specific patterns, let's discuss some fundamental concepts regarding scales and how they're used.

Why Scales?

Do we need to learn about scales to make music? The short answer is *no*. In a book about guitar scales, this may seem an unexpected answer. The truth is, creating music can be as simple as playing something you like the sound of. This is, after all, how most of us judge music as listeners. The deciding factor isn't usually whether we can make sense of it theoretically, but simply whether we think it sounds good.

Scales will be of little help if we lose sight of the fact that music is ultimately a *creative* endeavor. Having said that, it would be a mistake to conclude that scales are therefore not important. In creating anything musical, we're already engaging with scales, whether or not we know it. Scales are the basis for everything we do on guitar. They're foundational to things like improvisation, songwriting, arranging, understanding theory, and building technique. For guitar players, scales are a vital part of the language of music.

Scales are an essential tool for understanding how things are connected on the guitar neck. Beyond the obvious benefit practicing scales holds for tasks like developing technique and finger dexterity, understanding scales is fundamental for fretboard navigation. Being able to play effortlessly in any position on the fretboard, regardless of the key, is the byproduct of a solid grounding in guitar scales.

Learning scales not only provides a framework to help communicate our musical ideas, but it also opens the door to new creative possibilities. The belief that theory somehow inhibits creativity is a misconception. In most cases, the reverse is likely true: A lack of understanding will stifle creative potential. Many guitarists feel stuck playing the same old patterns and licks simply because *they can't use what they don't know*. Creative freedom comes from engaging and experimenting with the fundamentals, not from ignoring them.

Understanding Scales

For many, the topic of guitar scales can be daunting. While this is a reflection of the sheer number of scales that exist, it's also symptomatic of the way scales are commonly taught. As guitar players, we tend to think of scales simply as *shapes* on the fretboard. Although this is helpful from a practical standpoint, it gives little indication of what they are and how we might apply them.

The best place to start in understanding scales is actually not to start with *scales* at all. While scales are foundational, *intervals* are the real building blocks of music. An interval is the distance from one note to another. Even a slight shift in this relationship can create an entirely different mood or feel. Major and minor chords, for example, are theoretically just one half step away from being the same chord. It's this slight movement in the middle interval (the flattened 3rd) that dramatically changes the chord's character:

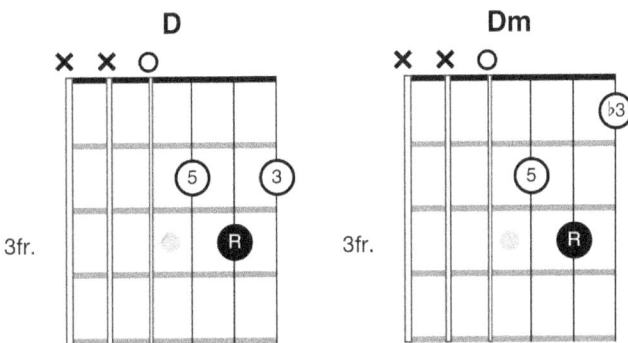

Simply put, a scale is a series of notes with *fixed* intervals. This means the structure these notes follow doesn't change, even when the scale is played in different keys. (This is why most scale shapes on guitar are movable.) It's this fixed sequence of intervals that evokes a scale's unique tonal flavor, or sonic personality, for composing or improvising. Like chords, scales can contain many of the same notes, but it's the slight differences that give a scale its distinct character.

In the Western world, there are only 12 notes in the musical alphabet. The endless creative options available to us come from the way we position these notes in relation to one another. Technically, we use patterns to visualize how notes can be grouped together on the fretboard. Creatively, however, it's more useful to think of a scale as describing a distinct *sound* or *mood*, rather than simply referring to a particular shape.

Tip: *Sometimes it's helpful to think about playing music in the same way we listen to it. When listening to music, we're not concentrating on shapes or positions; we're focused on sounds and emotions. While the technical aspects of learning an instrument are undeniably important, they're less significant than the ability to communicate something through the notes being played.*

Using Scales

As already established, guitar players tend to learn about scales *visually*. However, just being shown what they look like on the guitar fretboard doesn't actually help us use them. While scales are typically taught and practiced in ascending or descending sequences, this isn't how they're used in real-world situations. An audience will rarely care how many scales you know or how fast you can play them! The whole point of learning this information is to create something with it. Scales are simply the palette from which we express our musical ideas.

Guitar players are commonly confused about when and how to use scales. Unfortunately, scales aren't all that helpful if we don't understand how to apply them. In part, this confusion occurs because we're often taught to view chords and scales as separate entities that have different functions. A common example of this is the question: Do you play rhythm or lead guitar? While in a practical sense chords suit rhythm playing and scales suit lead playing, theoretically they're both derived from the same place. As already stated, *intervals* are the fundamental building blocks of music. We use them to create *both* melody and harmony. Chords and scales are therefore intrinsically related.

When we talk about playing in a particular key, we mean that notes used to construct chords and melodies relate to the same fixed sequence of intervals. A practical way to view this relationship would be to say that we build chords *using* scales. For example, all chords in the key of G major are built exclusively from notes within the G major scale and vice versa. This is why melodic ideas structured around the G major scale will work over a G major chord progression. They're both drawing on the same collection of common notes. It's this inherent chord/scale connection that forms the missing link where many players become confused.

To reiterate, scales are used to create both *rhythmic* and *melodic* structures. A songwriter will (knowingly or unknowingly) compose the melodic and harmonic elements of their song based on the mood or personality of a particular scale. As lead guitarists, our contribution to a song often comes after the chord progression has been established. Our task, then, is to find the appropriate scale (or *scales*) to base our melodic ideas on from notes within the chords being played.

Tip: *In many cases, this is relatively straightforward, since numerous progressions in popular music tend to stay within a single key center. However, it's not uncommon for a progression to temporarily borrow chords from another key signature or move to another key entirely. In these situations, our choice of scales needs to be informed by the specific chords being used, not just a single overall key center.*

Learning Scales

Before delving into the patterns covered in this guide, it makes sense first to lay down some ground rules. While there are no *overnight* solutions for learning scales on guitar, there are several learning habits that make this process much easier. In short, the task isn't simply about memorizing endless shapes on the fretboard. We want to understand how these patterns are built, how they function, and how they relate to one another. Below are some key guidelines to consider:

- **One at a Time:** Learning scales isn't a race! Focus on learning and using one shape at a time. It's far more beneficial knowing a handful of patterns really well than knowing many of them poorly. Ensure you can create something musical out of each shape before moving on to the next.

- **Play Slowly:** Playing scales *fast* isn't the initial goal; playing them *accurately* is. Start by practicing slowly at a comfortable tempo and increase speed only when each pattern can be played cleanly. Remember, playing *fast* is different from playing *badly at a fast tempo*.

- **Don't Practice Mistakes:** When we consistently practice something on guitar, we form playing habits. Pay attention to your playing and get used to correcting mistakes, not *practicing* them. Focus on playing things accurately, being mindful of both the tone and tuning of each note.

- **Learn to Self-Correct:** Rather than being frustrated by limitations, learn from them. These challenges teach us to see gaps in our understanding or issues with our technique. The roadblocks we encounter in our playing are signs telling us what to work on next.

- **Focus on Root Notes:** Always remember that we're learning scales, not just *shapes*. The root note forms the tonal center of a scale. As such, it's the central anchor point for our melodic ideas. Understanding the sound and structure of a scale is vital for applying it musically.

- **Look for Shortcuts:** While they can seem like endless amounts of information to memorize, in reality scale patterns include a large amount of repetition. Often, one shape will have multiple applications. Paying attention to these similarities will help streamline the learning process.

- **Make It Musical:** Scales don't always have to be practiced the same way. Make it interesting! Try alternating the rhythm, note sequence, tempo, or dynamics being used. Be sure to play along with songs or make use of jam tracks. Remember, learning scales is never the end goal—making music is.

- **Play in Context:** Don't just practice playing scales; practice hearing and using them *in context*. Listening to and experimenting with the ways other guitarists use these patterns musically is essential for developing your own creative vocabulary on guitar.

- **Repetition Is Key:** Learning scales isn't a difficult task, but it's a *repetitive* one. Consistent practice is key. Be sure to prioritize shorter, more regular practice sessions over longer, more infrequent ones.

- **Be Intentional:** Sometimes, learning something effectively isn't just about the time we spend; it's about *how* we spend our time. Ultimately, focused practice is efficient practice. Be mindful of each specific thing you're looking to improve, and then structure your practice time accordingly.

2

Octave Shapes

Having covered some foundational concepts for learning and using scales, we'll now introduce five key reference points for working with these patterns on the fretboard.

Using Octave Shapes

As already stated, this handbook relates to the various patterns rooted in the diatonic world. Another way of saying this is that each scale and arpeggio covered is connected to the major scale. This is a simple yet extremely important concept to grasp. While scales and arpeggios are often learned or memorized as *unrelated* patterns, this isn't how they function. A pentatonic scale, for example, is basically the major scale minus a few notes. Similarly, both modes and arpeggios are also formed from notes within the major scale.

In short, these shapes are all closely related. While each pattern can be used in isolation, it's important to learn how they overlap and interconnect with one another on the fretboard. Failing to understand this will introduce roadblocks in navigating these patterns effectively when improvising or songwriting. One of the biggest problems in learning to visualize scale shapes as separate patterns is that it's easy to lose sight of how to connect them back up again. Fortunately, there's a simple solution to this problem. It starts with focusing on how each pattern is *similar* before outlining what makes them distinct.

For example, the A minor scale, A minor pentatonic scale, and A minor arpeggio all contain overlapping notes. Here we're primarily interested in the foundational note common to all these shapes, the root note A. While these patterns form distinct shapes on the fretboard, they all revolve around the same starting point. Therefore, even though the overall shape of each pattern will change, the shape created by the root notes within each pattern will not.

Why is this important to understand? Simply put, root notes are foundational to the structure of any scale or arpeggio. In the following section, we'll see that when any note is mapped out across the fretboard, it creates *five* unique octave shapes. These distinct shapes remain consistent, regardless of our starting note. Therefore, it's logical that any scale or arpeggio must be built around one of these five shapes. This will be true no matter what key we're playing in or our position on the fretboard.

As such, all patterns demonstrated in the following chapters of this book will be anchored to one of these octave shapes. This means that each octave shape acts as a basic reference point for visualizing how the numerous patterns covered relate to one another. Understanding this fact enables us to creatively interchange between using modes with pentatonic scales and arpeggios when playing in particular areas on the fretboard.

Tip: Learning where the root notes are positioned within each scale or arpeggio provides a visual anchor for understanding how these patterns overlap and interconnect. This concept is often discussed in reference to the CAGED system, as these octave shapes also form the basis of our basic C, A, G, E, and D open chords.

Octave Shapes

Position 1

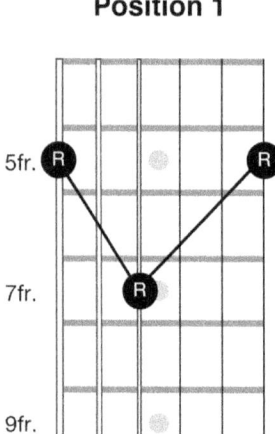

Position 2

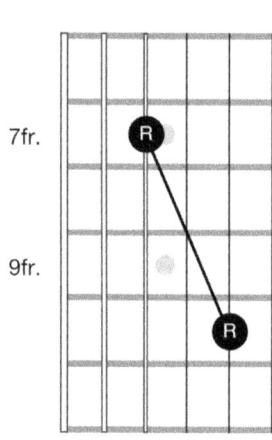

Position 3

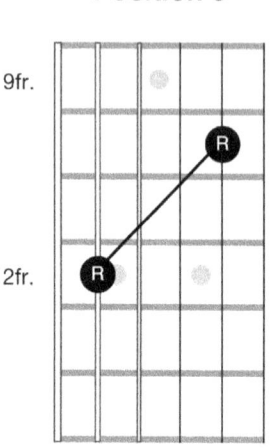

Position 4

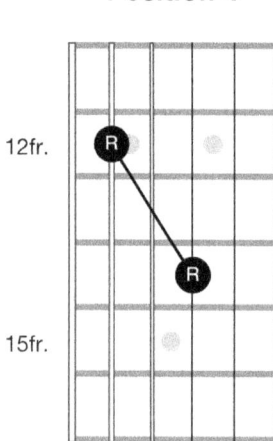

Position 5

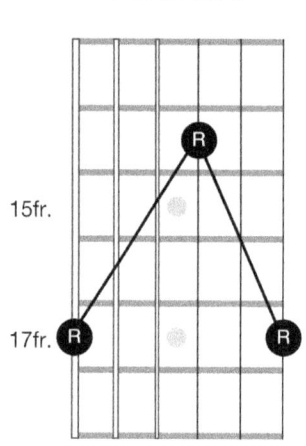

3

Modes

Now that we've covered the groundwork, let's continue by discussing the modes of the major scale.

Understanding Modes

In this chapter, we'll start by looking at the seven modes of the major scale. These patterns form an important foundation for understanding both music theory and fretboard navigation. As such, they'll provide the fundamental framework for exploring all the other diatonic patterns covered in this book. Here's a brief overview describing the structure and sound of each scale.

Note: *Type* refers to the overall tonality of the scale. *Formula* explains the intervallic structure of the scale. *Structure* describes the half-step (one-fret) and whole-step (two-fret) movements within the scale. And *description* briefly outlines the unique tonal character of the scale.

The Ionian Mode (Major Scale)

- **Type:** Major
- **Formula:** R - 2 - 3 - 4 - 5 - 6 - 7
- **Structure:** W - W - H - W - W - W - H
- **Description:** More commonly known as the *major* scale, the Ionian mode is the parent scale to all other modes. Sonically, it has a familiar, triumphant, and cheerful quality.

The Dorian Mode

- **Type:** Minor
- **Formula:** R - 2 - ♭3 - 4 - 5 - 6 - ♭7
- **Structure:** W - H - W - W - W - H - W
- **Description:** Built from the 2nd note (or *degree*) of the major scale, the Dorian mode is essentially a minor scale without the flattened 6th interval. While this mode is categorized as minor, it has a distinctly brighter, bluesier tonality.

The Phrygian Mode

- **Type:** Minor
- **Formula:** R - ♭2 - ♭3 - 4 - 5 - ♭6 - ♭7
- **Structure:** H - W - W - W - H - W - W
- **Description:** Built from the 3rd degree of the major scale, the Phrygian mode is essentially a minor scale with a flattened 2nd. This mode sounds dark and exotic; it's often described as having a uniquely Spanish sound.

The Lydian Mode

- **Type:** Major
- **Formula:** R - 2 - 3 - ♯4 - 5 - 6 - 7
- **Structure:** W - W - W - H - W - W - H
- **Description:** Built from the 4th degree of the major scale, the Lydian mode is essentially a major scale with a raised 4th. The Lydian mode is often described as having a mysterious and dreamy quality.

The Mixolydian Mode

- **Type:** Major
- **Formula:** R - 2 - 3 - 4 - 5 - 6 - ♭7
- **Structure:** W - W - H - W - W - H - W
- **Description:** Built from the 5th degree of the major scale, the Mixolydian mode is essentially a major scale with a flattened 7th. Sometimes called the *dominant* mode, it sounds similar to the major scale, just with a slightly funkier tonality.

The Aeolian Mode (Minor Scale)

- **Type:** Minor

- **Formula:** R - 2 - ♭3 - 5 - 4 - ♭6 - ♭7

- **Structure:** W - H - W - W - H - W - W

- **Description:** Built from the 6th degree of the major scale, the Aeolian mode is usually referred to as the *minor* or *natural minor* scale. This mode is known for its dramatic or moody sonic quality.

The Locrian Mode

- **Type:** Diminished

- **Formula:** R - ♭2 - ♭3 - 4 - ♭5 - ♭6 - ♭7

- **Structure:** H - W - W - H - W - W - W

- **Description:** Built from the 7th degree of the major scale, the Locrian mode is sometimes called the *half-diminished* mode. It has a dissonant and unstable sound and as such is the least widely used of all the modes.

Using Modes

The modes are commonly misunderstood; they're a popular subject of confusion and debate. Like the pentatonic scales we'll look at, the modes can be broadly categorized under two main types: *major* and *minor* (with the exception of the Locrian mode). Unlike pentatonic scales, however, modal scales are more nuanced and detailed in their tonal character. While this isn't intended to be a detailed theoretical guide, here we'll attempt to ease some of the confusion around this subject.

First, let's clarify the term *modes*. What we're actually referring to are the modes of the *major scale*. This indicates that there's an intrinsic relationship between each modal pattern. Seen from the simplest standpoint, modes are essentially different *inversions* of the same major scale. The mode just refers to our starting point within that scale. For example, the second mode of C major (D Dorian) uses the same notes, but it starts and ends on the 2nd degree of the scale. Put simply, it's the same scale played from a different position.

> *Tip:* Why is knowing this helpful? Because we can get considerably more mileage from a single scale. Learning to navigate the alternate positions of the major scale allows us to play in any key, from any point along the entire guitar neck!

In this context, the modes are viewed *relative* to one another. This is usually how they're applied over major and minor chord progressions that stay within one key center. In these situations, practically speaking, there's no real sonic distinction between one mode and another. They each function more as alternate positions of each other, rather than as distinct scales in their own right. For example, playing the third mode of C major (E Phrygian) over a C major progression will still basically sound like the C major scale.

So if each mode uses the same notes, what makes them sound different? Theoretically, because each mode has a different starting point, this shift in the intervals gives each scale a different sound. However, in practice, the distinct character of each mode is apparent only when chords and melodies are structured to emphasize this new *tonal center*. In simple terms, this means the tonality of a scale will change depending on the chords being played. For example, you'll often hear modes being used over a static chord to emphasize their unique sonic quality (e.g., D Dorian over a Dm chord vamp).

Similarly, diatonic progressions can be structured to emphasize the sound of any one of the modes. Here a progression uses the chords of the parent major key but *implies* the sound of a particular mode by revolving around an alternate root (or *tonic*) chord within the scale. Again, the notes being used are the same, but the tonal center being emphasized is different. For example, implying the sound of F major using only the notes and chords from the C major scale would give us an F Lydian sound (F being the 4th degree of C major). This provides a distinctly different sonic quality to a standard F major scale.

Non-diatonic situations are where things get even more interesting. Where a progression moves outside a singular key center, modal scales are commonly used in *parallel* with one another. For example, if a progression were to change key from C to G, the scale used would also need to change to reflect this shift. It may seem obvious just to play the major scales attached to each key center (C major to G major). When playing, however, jumping around to different positions on the fretboard isn't a practical solution. Instead, using the mode of G major that most closely relates to C (the fifth mode, C Mixolydian) provides a much smoother transition. C major and C Mixolydian are similar scales; they start from the same root note, share many common tones, and occupy the same space on the fretboard. This means they can seamlessly interchange with one another.

Finally, a more advanced use of this parallel concept can include *superimposing* one mode where another would be more expected. This involves temporarily substituting one parallel mode for another, not to navigate a key change but to add further tension and interest where desired. Using an E Dorian scale for a *bluesier* sound over an E7 chord (which usually implies the sound of E Mixolydian) would be an example of this. Keep in mind that while this concept certainly adds a different flavor to your melodic ideas, if done carelessly the results can be unpleasant.

Summary

To recap, despite not being a comprehensive overview of the modes, this has hopefully clarified some of the ways they're often used. We can summarize these common applications for modes as follows:

- **Used Over Diatonic Progressions:** Modal patterns are commonly used to play over any major or minor progression that stays within a single key center.

- **Used Over Single-Chord Vamps:** The modes are often applied over a single-chord vamp, where a static chord is used to emphasize the tonal center of a particular modal scale.

- **Used Over Modal Progressions:** Modal scales are often used over diatonic progressions that center around an alternate tonic chord, implying the sound of one key by using the notes and chords from another key.

- **Used Over Key Changes:** The modes can be used to seamlessly navigate through key changes within a song, without jumping around to alternate positions on the fretboard.

- **Used in Parallel:** Substituting one parallel mode (a different mode starting from the same root note) over another is a device used to add further interest or color to a melodic pattern where desired.

Tip: *Notice that despite the various diagrams following this section, each mode repeats the same seven patterns on the fretboard. The only thing that changes is the tonal center of each pattern. For example, over an A minor progression, the C major scale will sound like A minor. Logically, if our melodic ideas gravitate to the sound of A minor, it makes sense that A is the root note, not C.*

Playing Modes

Modal scales can be played in various ways across the fretboard. Here we'll favor an approach that uses three notes per string. Not only do these shapes give us greater reach within a single position, but they also accommodate increased speed and fluidity in our playing. Below we can use the A major scale to demonstrate what this approach looks like when ascending and descending through the root position.

Example 3.1

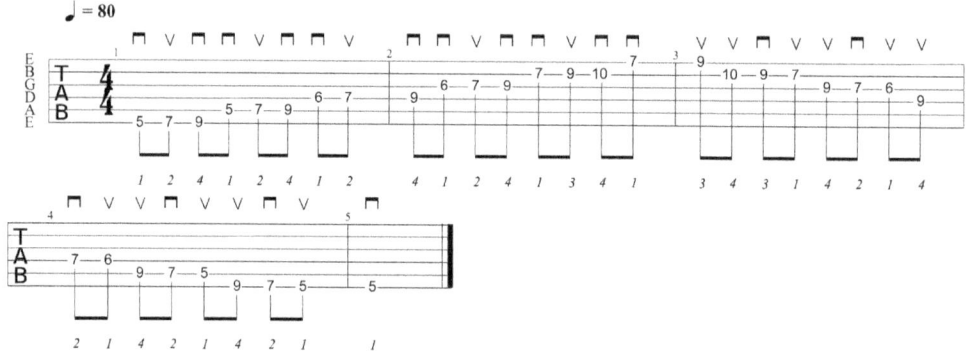

Finger Position

This pattern highlights the three basic movements our left hand will encounter when playing three notes per string. These are:

- Three notes separated by a whole step each (W - W).

- Three notes separated by a half step and then a whole step (H - W).

- Three notes separated by a whole step and then a half step (W - H).

In these situations, the suggested fingerings are:

- Using the 1st, 2nd, and 4th fingers for both W - W and H - W movements.

- Using the 1st, 3rd, and 4th fingers for W - H movements.

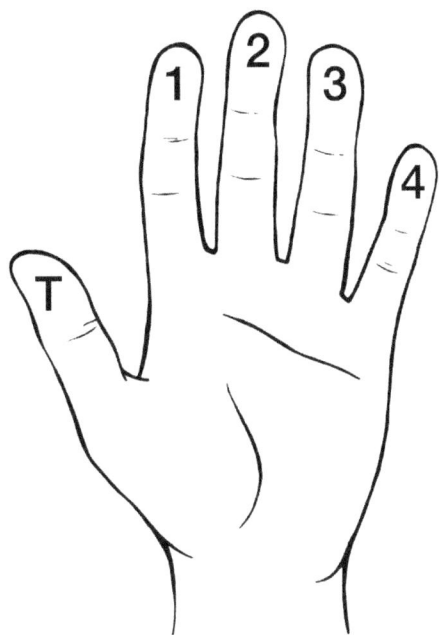

Note: Three-note-per-string shapes might feel foreign at first. Initially, it may be helpful to practice playing these scales higher on the neck, where the fret spacing is closer.

Picking Technique

While standard downstrokes/upstrokes (or *alternate* picking) could be used with these patterns, the previous example demonstrates a different approach. *Economy* picking is a popular technique applied to sequences using three notes per string. It allows us to play consecutive downstrokes when ascending from one string to another and consecutive upstrokes when descending the alternate way. This enables us to omit unnecessary movements from our picking technique, maximizing both accuracy and speed.

The Ionian Mode

Position 1

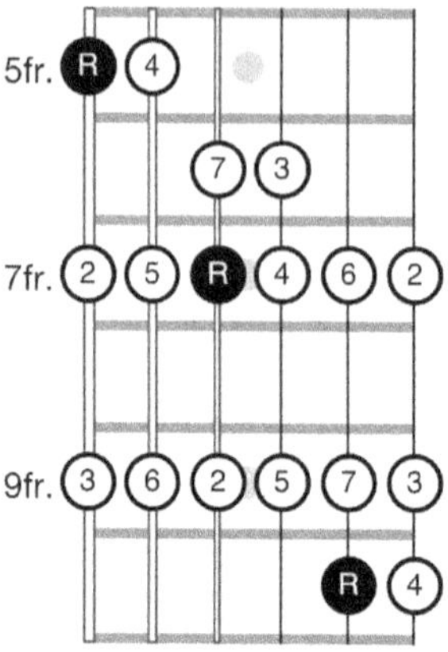

Position 2

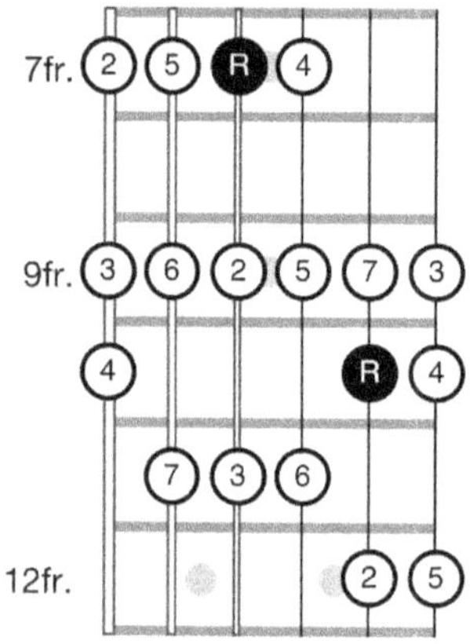

Position 3

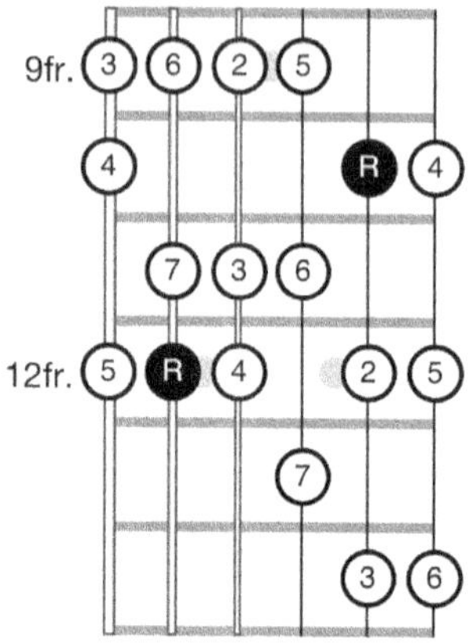

Position 4

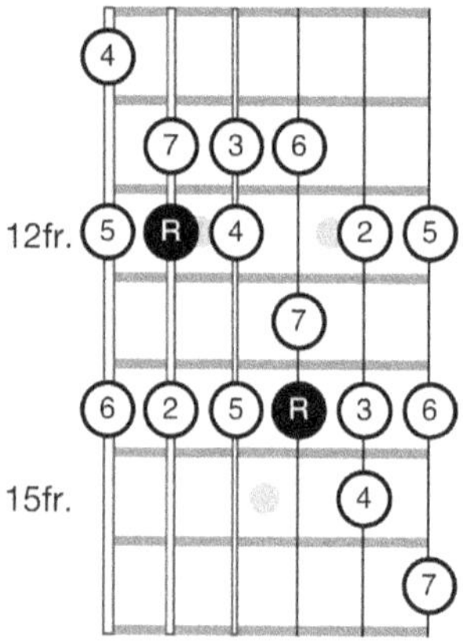

Position 5

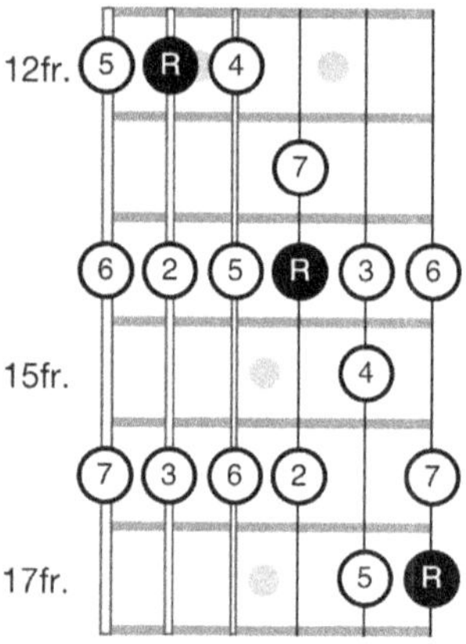

Position 6

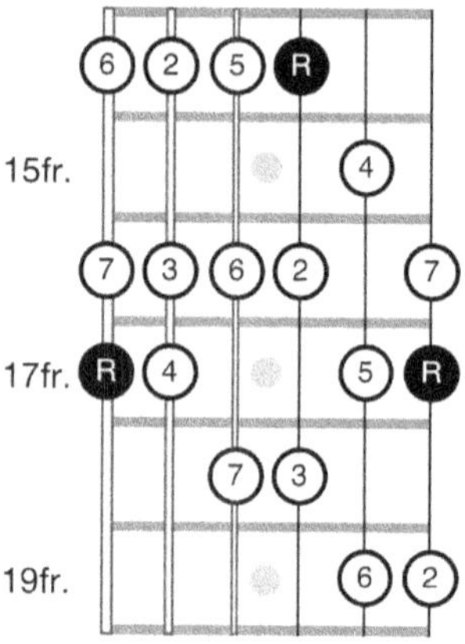

Position 7

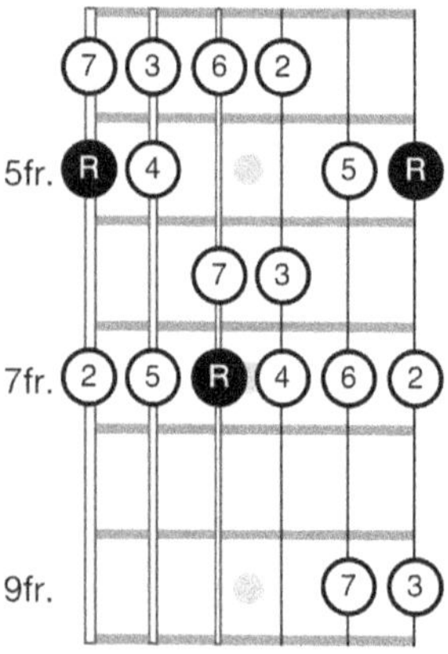

The Dorian Mode

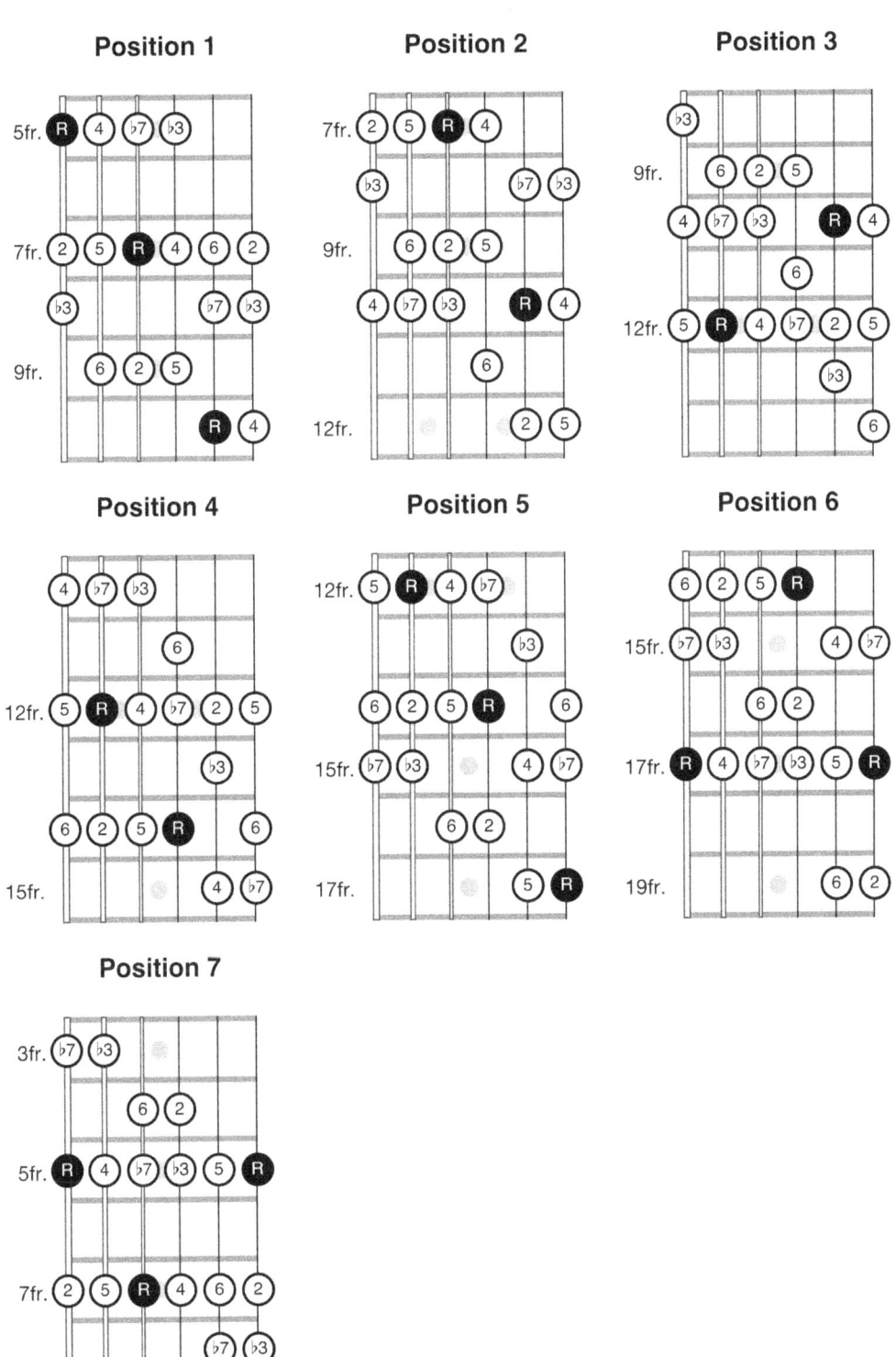

The Phrygian Mode

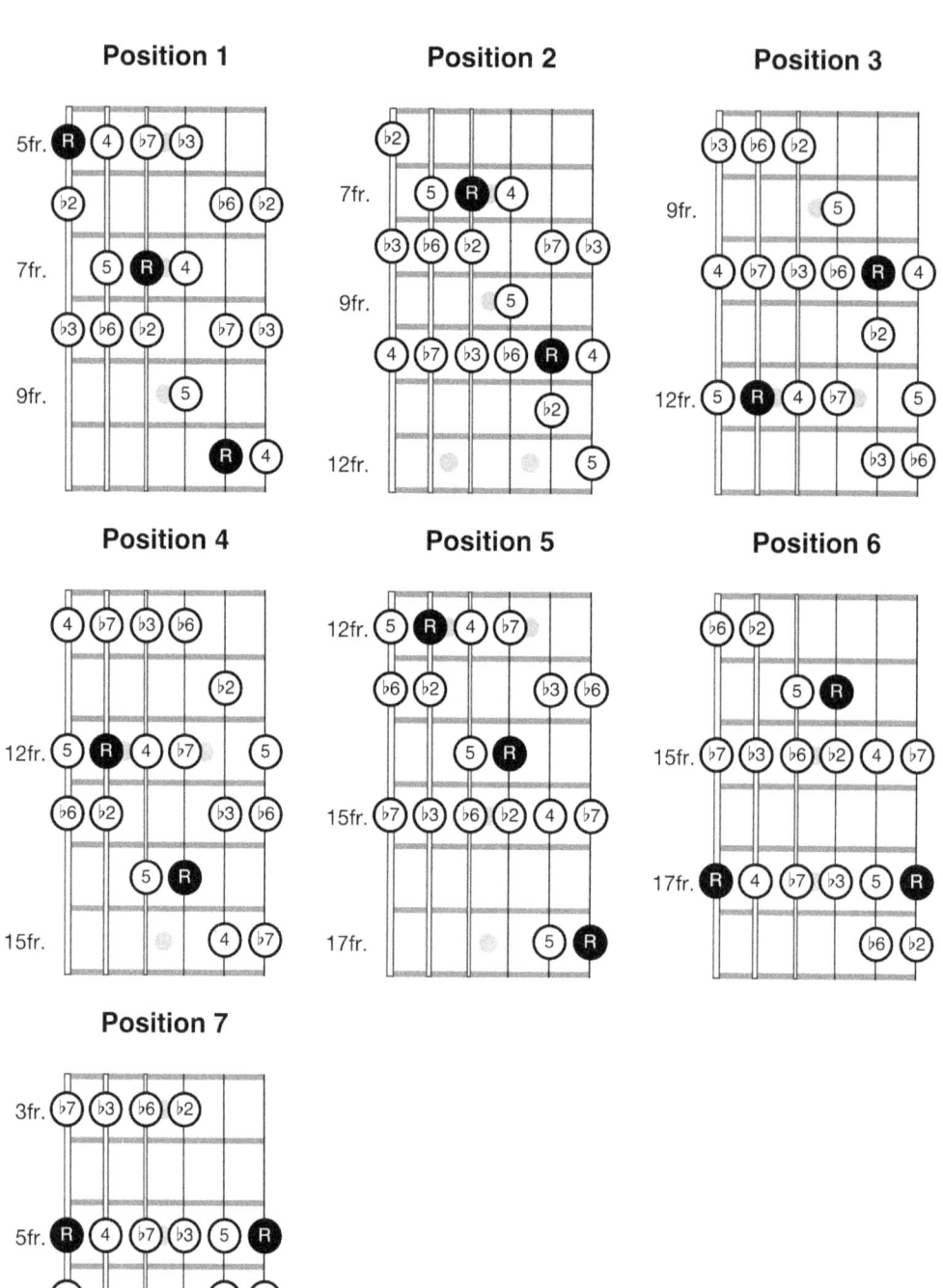

The Lydian Mode

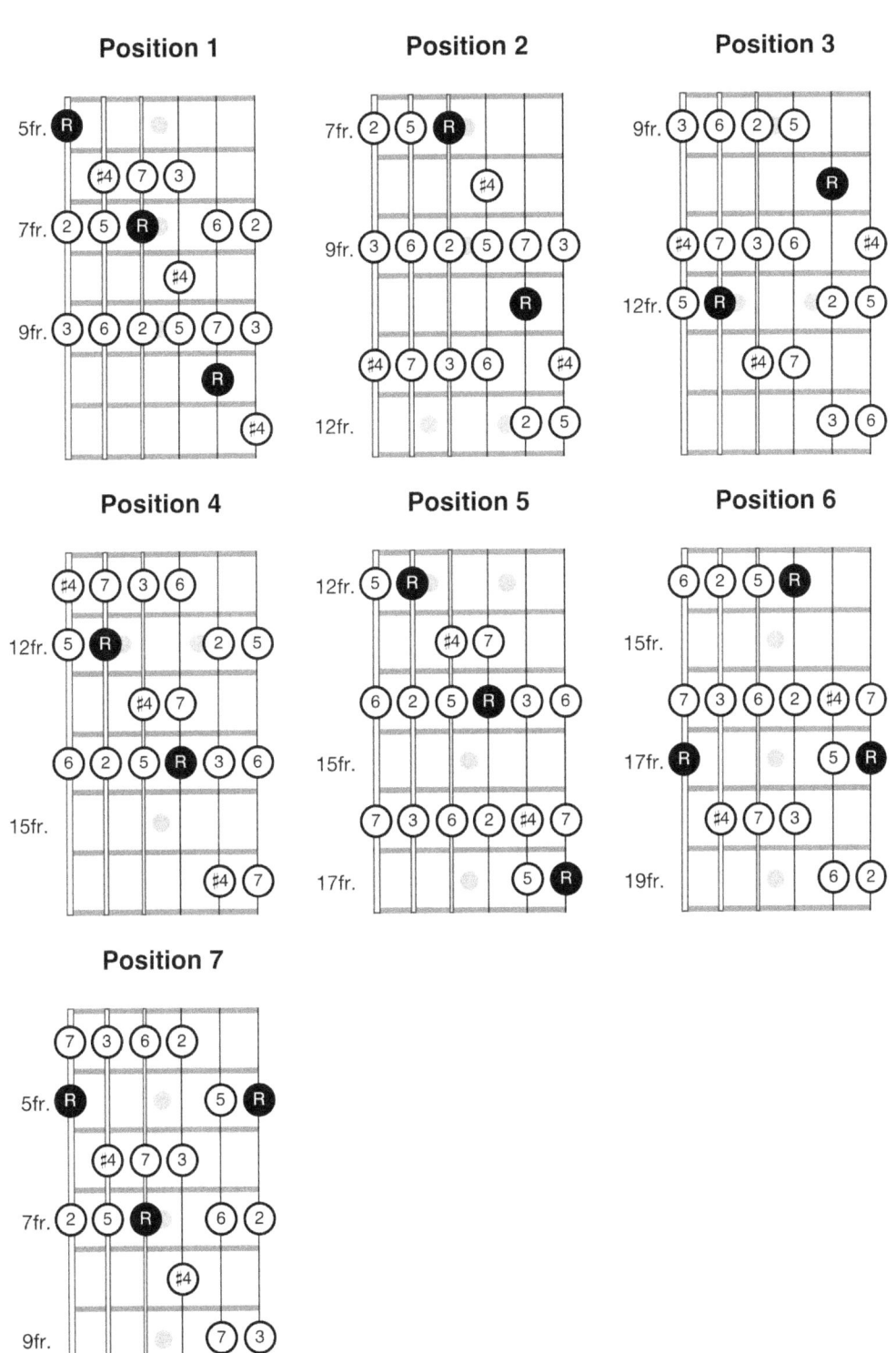

The Mixolydian Mode

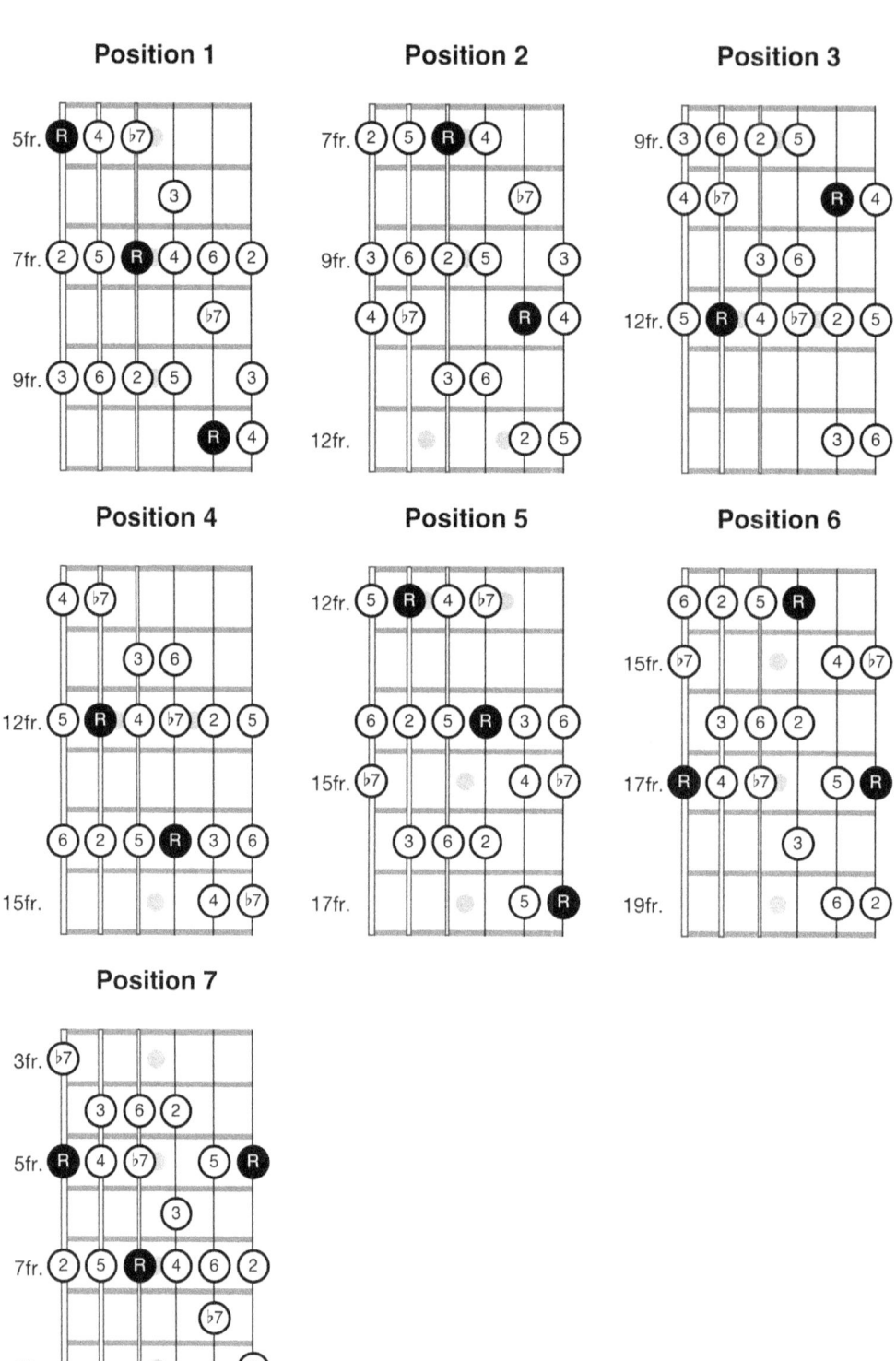

The Aeolian Mode

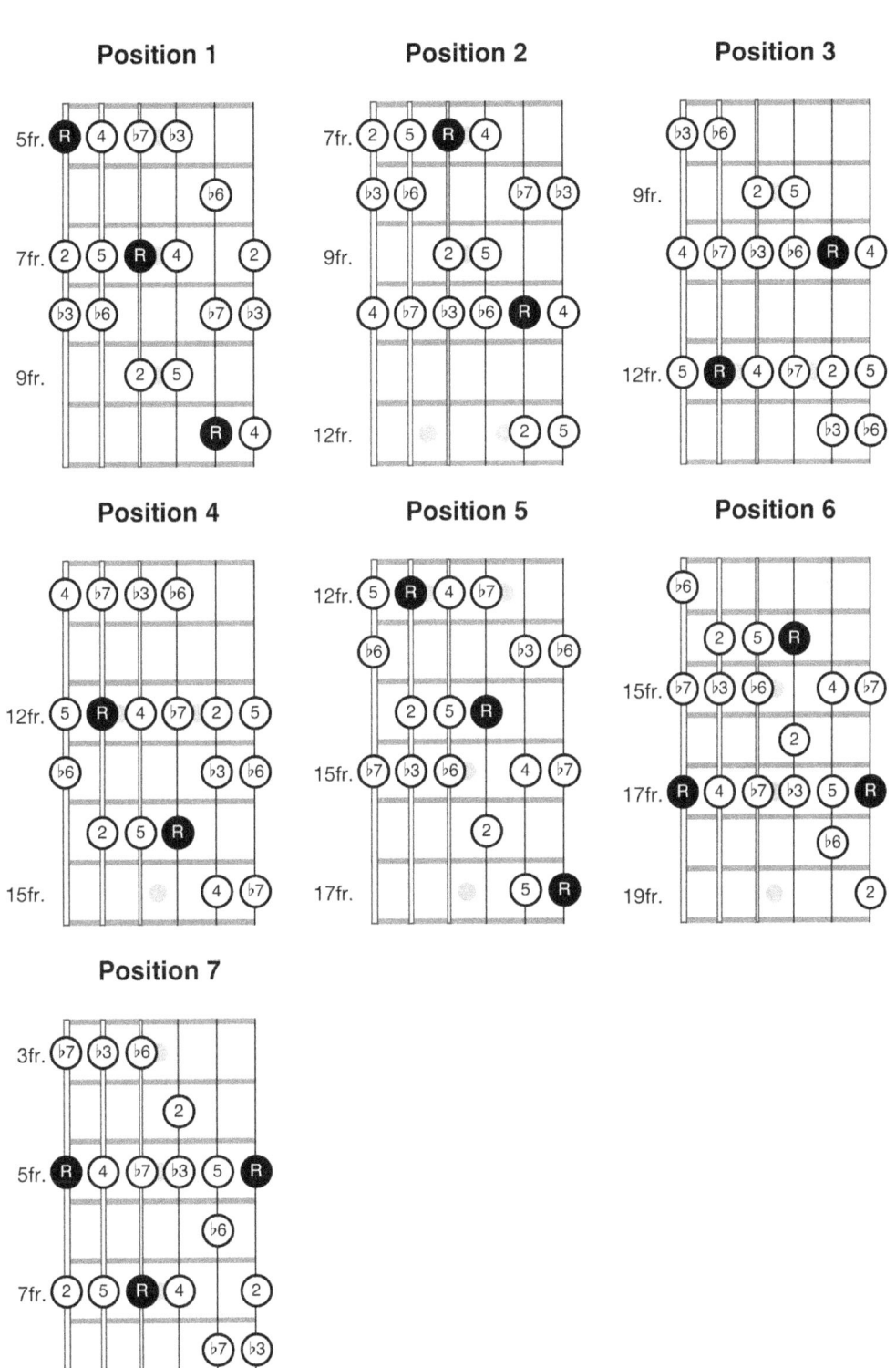

The Locrian Mode

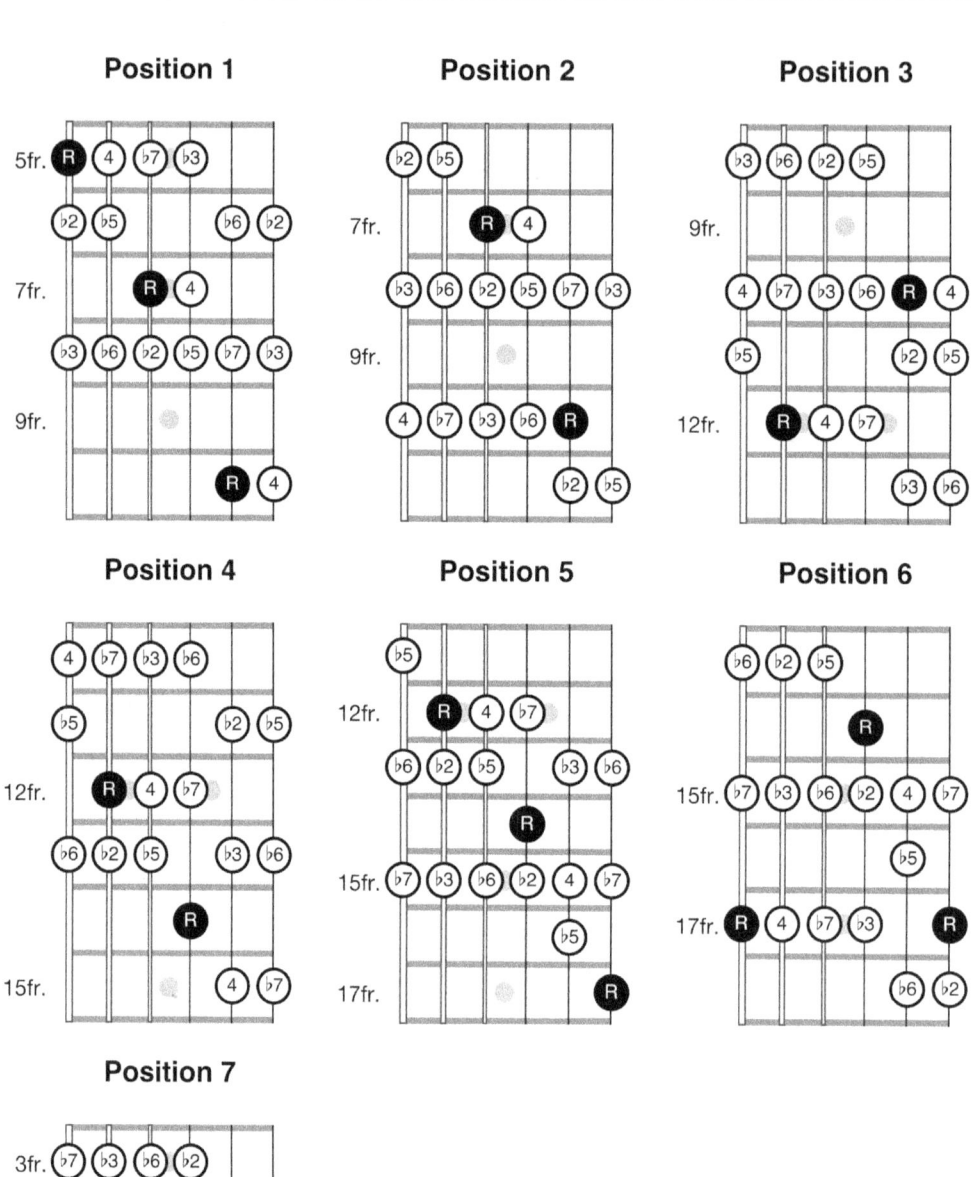

Exercise 1

Start at the 1st position of the major or minor scale and loop through its *relative* positions on the fretboard.

Using a metronome, start at the 3rd fret and play up and back through the G major scale (Ionian) at a comfortable tempo. Repeat this with each subsequent position of G major until you reach the root position again (one octave higher at the 15th fret). After playing once through all seven positions, reverse this exercise to loop through each pattern until you arrive back at the 1st position on the 3rd fret.

Now, repeat this same exercise in the key of G minor. Again, start from the 3rd fret, but this time cycle through each position of the G minor scale (Aeolian).

*Tip: It's highly recommended that you finish each position by playing through the root notes in that pattern. This is very helpful for reinforcing a position's connection with its relative octave shape (covered in **Chapter 2**).*

Exercise 2

Start at the 1st position of the major or minor scale and loop through its *parallel* positions on the fretboard.

Using a metronome, start at the 5th fret and play up and back through the A major scale. Continue by playing through each subsequent mode in *parallel* (e.g., A Dorian, A Phrygian, A Lydian, etc.). Once you have played all seven shapes in parallel, reverse this exercise and loop back through each pattern until you arrive back at the A major scale.

Extra Credit

- Experiment with playing **Exercise 1** using not only the major and minor scales but all the other modes as well. Starting at the 3rd fret, loop through each position of every mode (e.g., G Dorian, G Phrygian, G Lydian, etc.).

- Play **Exercise 1** and **Exercise 2** but avoid ascending and descending through the same position. In other words, try ascending through one pattern and then descending through the next pattern continually in an alternate sequence.

Note: The exercises in this book focus on fretboard navigation. They're designed to work with multiple patterns and positions together. It may take time concentrating on each pattern separately before you can incorporate these larger exercises into your practice.

4

Pentatonic Scales

Having established a broad framework for navigating the fretboard using modes, it's time to explore how this relates to pentatonic scales.

Understanding Pentatonic Scales

In this chapter, we'll discuss the use of pentatonic scales. While, technically, blues scales wouldn't be considered *pentatonic* scales (*penta* implying five notes), they're so commonly used interchangeably with pentatonic scales that it makes sense to include them here. Below is a brief description of each pattern we'll cover:

The Major Pentatonic Scale

- **Type:** Major
- **Formula:** R - 2 - 3 - 5 - 6
- **Structure:** W - W - W+H - W
- **Description:** The major pentatonic scale is essentially a major scale minus the 4th and 7th degrees. It maintains an overall *major* tonality, but the absence of these half-step movements gives this scale a more open sound.

The Major Blues Scale

- **Type:** Major
- **Formula:** R - 2 - ♭3 - 3 - 5 - 6
- **Structure:** W - H - H - W+H - W
- **Description:** Arguably not as popular as the minor blues scale, the major blues scale uses the same notes as a major pentatonic scale, with the addition of a flattened 3rd. Usually used as a passing note, this chromatic tone gives the scale additional color and tension.

The Minor Pentatonic Scale

- **Type:** Minor
- **Formula:** R - ♭3 - 4 - 5 - ♭7
- **Structure:** W+H - W - W - W+H
- **Description:** The minor pentatonic scale is essentially a minor scale minus the 2nd and 6th degrees. As with the major pentatonic, omitting these half-step movements gives the minor pentatonic scale a broader sound.

The Minor Blues Scale

- **Type:** Minor
- **Formula:** R - ♭3 - 4 - ♭5 - 5 - ♭7
- **Structure:** W+H - W - H - H - W+H
- **Description:** Often referred to simply as the *blues scale*, the minor blues scale uses the notes of its minor pentatonic counterpart but adds a flattened 5th. Like the major blues scale, this passing note gives the scale a significantly bluesier character.

Note: Unlike all the other scales and arpeggios covered in this book, blues scales contain non-diatonic notes. In other words, these are *chromatic* notes not found within either parent major or minor scales.

Using Pentatonic Scales

Pentatonic scales are used extensively throughout numerous genres. They're often the first stop for most aspiring lead guitarists. Not only are they easier to play and understand than modal scales, but the lack of any half-step intervals also makes them better suited to wider applications. While this means they're extremely useful, pentatonic scales lack the tonal nuances we find within the modes.

Pentatonic scales are commonly used in place of (or in conjunction with) their parent major or minor scales when improvising or composing. As already mentioned, they're also often used interchangeably with blues scales. While the name may suggest an exclusive association with blues music, this scale is used widely throughout various other genres such as rock and jazz. In practice, this interchange isn't usually viewed as substituting one scale type for another. Rather, it's seen as incorporating colorful *passing notes* from the blues scales to embellish our pentatonic licks and ideas.

Not only are pentatonic scales commonly used to play over an entire progression, but they can also be applied independently over different chords. This involves structuring melodic phrases around multiple pentatonic scales to align with each major or minor chord change in a progression. Using a single pentatonic scale will emphasize the overall tonal center of a progression, whereas using multiple scales will better outline the sound of each specific chord.

Note: Like the octave shapes covered in **Chapter 2**, this technique of connecting pentatonic patterns with individual chord shapes is often referred to as part of the CAGED system.

Additionally, pentatonic scales can be used with other modal scales outside the parent major or minor scales. For example, the major pentatonic scale can be used interchangeably with any of the major modes: Ionian, Lydian, and Mixolydian. Likewise, the minor pentatonic scale can be substituted with any of the minor modes: Dorian, Phrygian, and Aeolian. This is possible because the intervals that differentiate these modes from one another are helpfully omitted in the major and minor pentatonic scales. In other words, pentatonic scales share the same intervals common to each mode, in both major and minor contexts.

Tip: Pentatonic scales are great for navigating through chord progressions when you're unsure of the exact mode to use. This is partly why they're so popular, because they work so well in various situations.

Theoretically, for the more advanced player, this concept opens the door to some interesting *substitutions*. When playing over a particular key center, we could technically use pentatonic scales based on any mode within that key. For example, this means that over a C major progression, we could play a *C major* pentatonic scale from the tonic (based on Ionian), an *F major* pentatonic scale from the 4th degree (based on Lydian), or a *G major* pentatonic scale from the 5th degree (based on Mixolydian). All without moving outside notes in the parent major scale! The same concept would also apply when playing in a minor key. However, it's worth noting that while they add some interesting color, substituted pentatonic scales usually sound less *resolved* than those based on the tonic chord of a progression.

This concept of pentatonic substitution can be extended even further. *Parallel* pentatonic scales are commonly used to intentionally move outside what might typically be considered the *safe* notes to play over a chord progression. Examples of this include using minor pentatonic scales over major chords or temporarily substituting parallel major and minor pentatonic scales in place of one another. Both examples are extremely common in blues music.

Summary

While this wasn't intended to be a thorough analysis of pentatonic theory, it has hopefully provided insight into the usefulness and versatility the humble pentatonic scale provides. To summarize, we can recap their popular applications as follows:

- **Used Over Diatonic Progressions:** Pentatonic scales are commonly used in place of their parent major and minor scales when playing over an entire chord progression.

- **Used Over Chord Changes:** Pentatonic scales are often used to emphasize the chord changes in a progression by matching the corresponding pentatonic pattern to each major or minor chord shape.

- **Used Instead of Modes:** Pentatonic scales can be used in place of any major or minor mode, because they're built using the common tones between these scales.

- **Used in Substitution:** Using the modal positions as a reference, various pentatonic scales can be substituted over a single key center, without moving outside the key.

- **Used in Parallel:** Often used for its *bluesy* tonality, parallel major and minor pentatonic scales are commonly played interchangeably for added flavor to melodic ideas.

Tip: Like the modes, both major and minor pentatonic scales use the same patterns on the fretboard; they just start from different positions. In either context, the tonal center or root note is the only thing that changes, not the actual shape.

Playing Pentatonic Scales

It's possible to play pentatonic scales in various ways on the fretboard. By far the most popular method, however, uses five basic *box* shapes. The larger interval gaps in pentatonic scales make them well suited to playing two notes per string (with the exception of additional notes in the blues patterns). While these shapes are arguably less conducive to speed picking, they're easier to play than modal patterns. Below, we can use the A major pentatonic scale to demonstrate what this approach looks like when ascending and descending through the root position.

Example 4.1

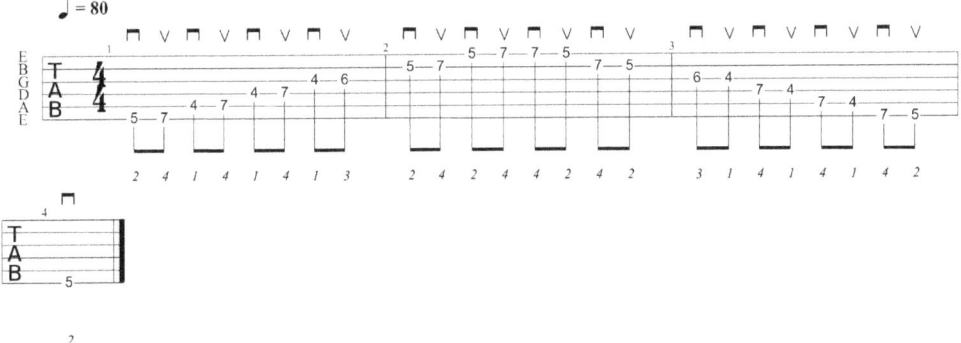

Finger Position

This pattern highlights the two basic movements our left hand will encounter when playing two notes per string in this way. These are:

- Two notes separated by a whole step (W).

- Two notes separated by a whole step plus a half step (W + H).

In these situations, common fingerings include:

- Using the 1st and 3rd fingers for W movements.

- Using the 1st and 4th fingers for W + H movements.

Note: Since pentatonic scales are each contained within a four-fret area on the fretboard, you could alternatively allocate each finger to cover one fret (as demonstrated in the example). In reality, though, once you're familiar with each basic pattern, fingerings often change intuitively depending on what's being played. This is especially true when using additional notes from the blues scales, as these tend to move out of the four-fret box shape.

Picking Technique

Here, alternate picking has been suggested. However, the economy picking technique outlined in **Chapter 3** can be used on select strings when adding notes from the blues scales.

Major Pentatonic Scales

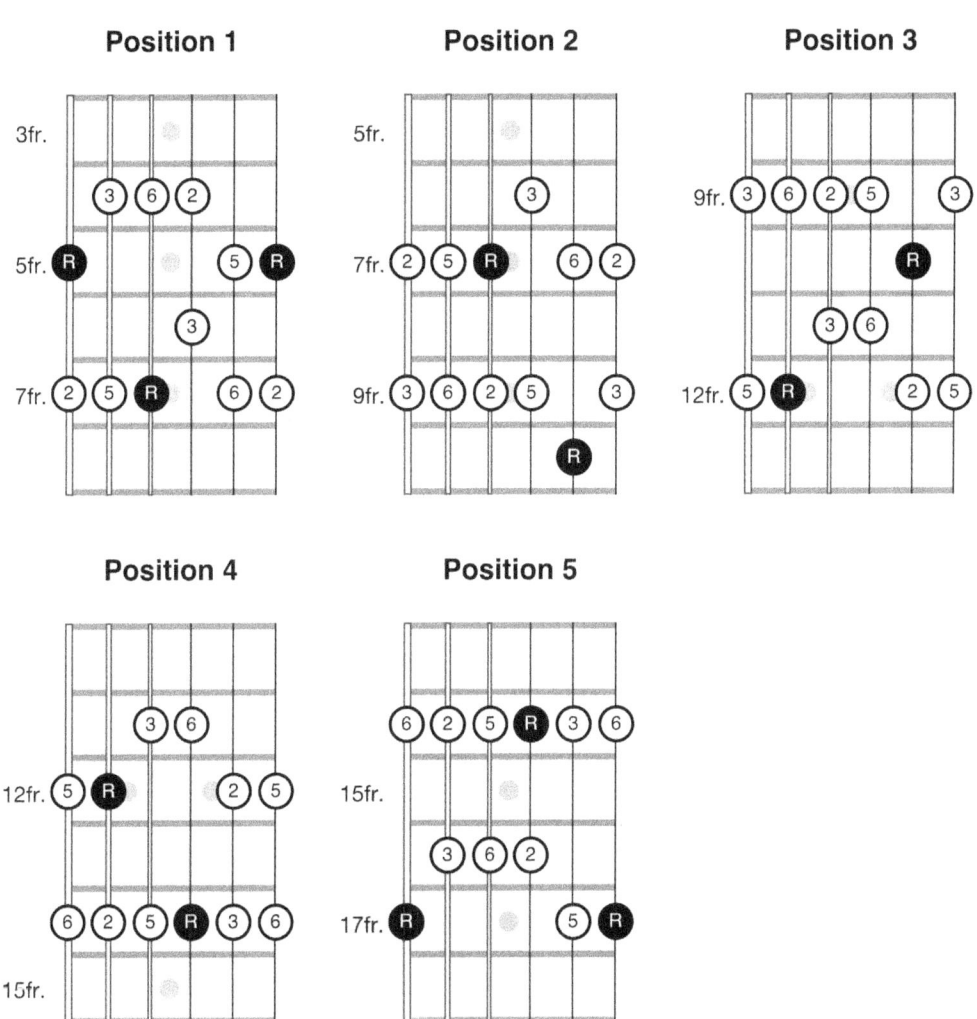

Major Blues Scales

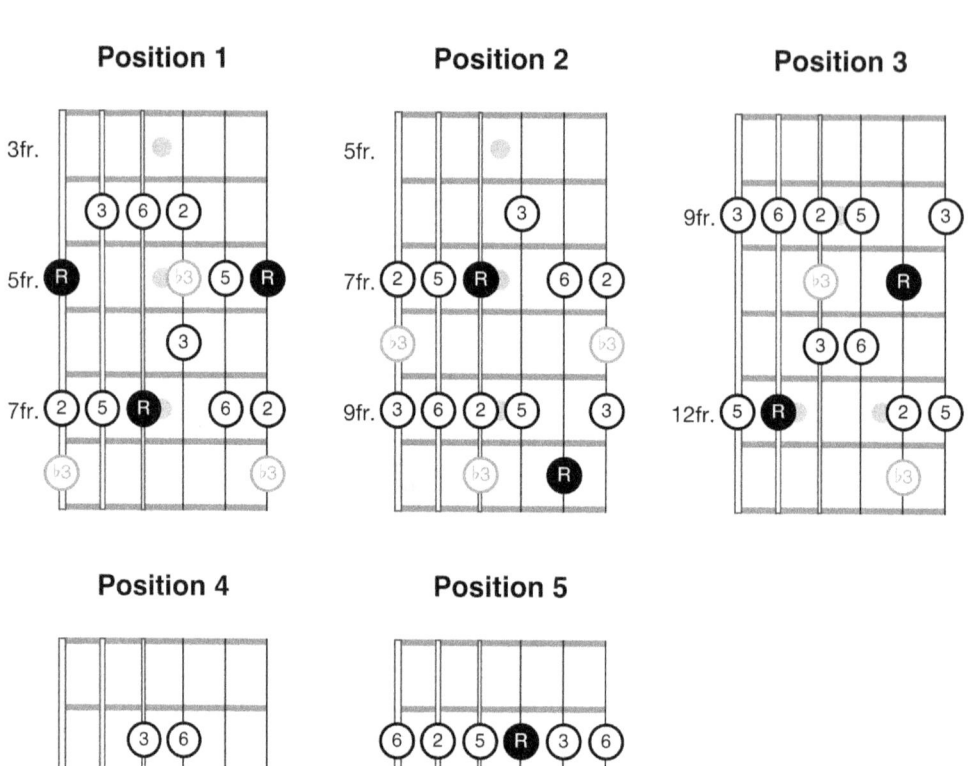

Minor Pentatonic Scales

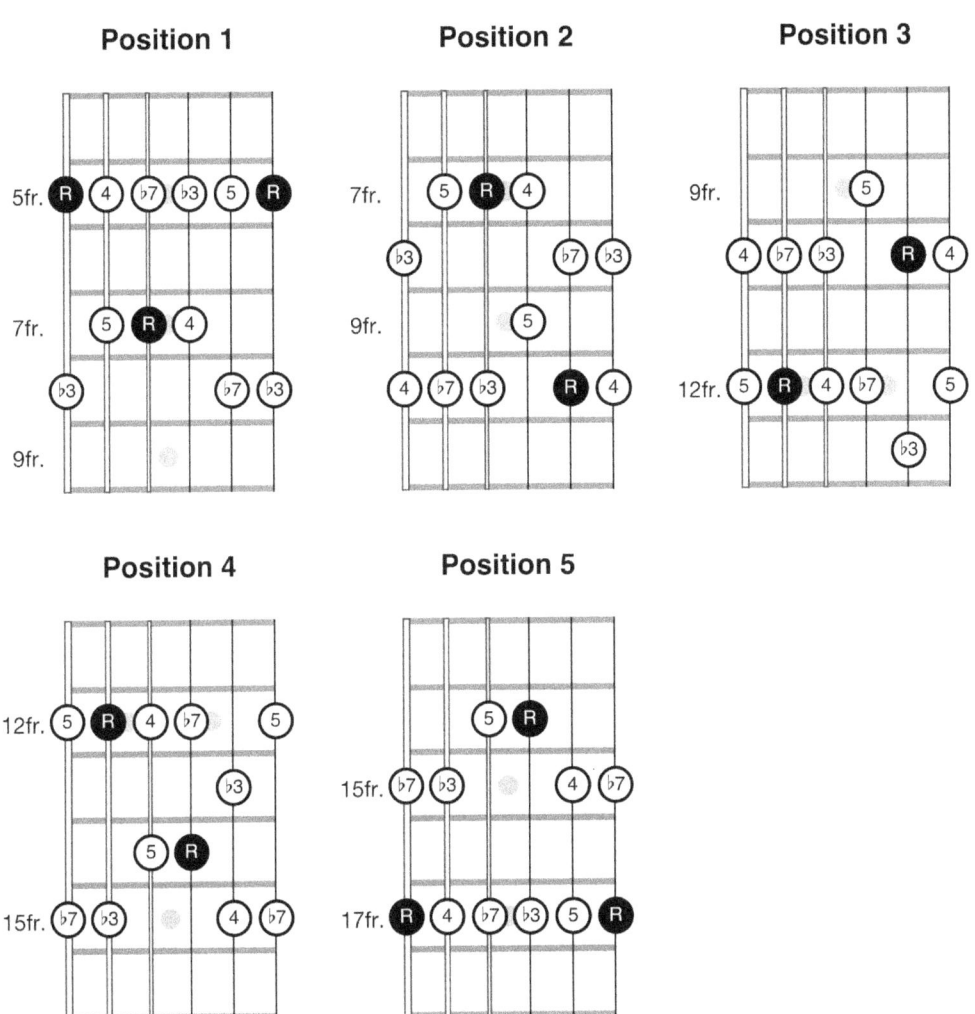

Minor Blues Scales

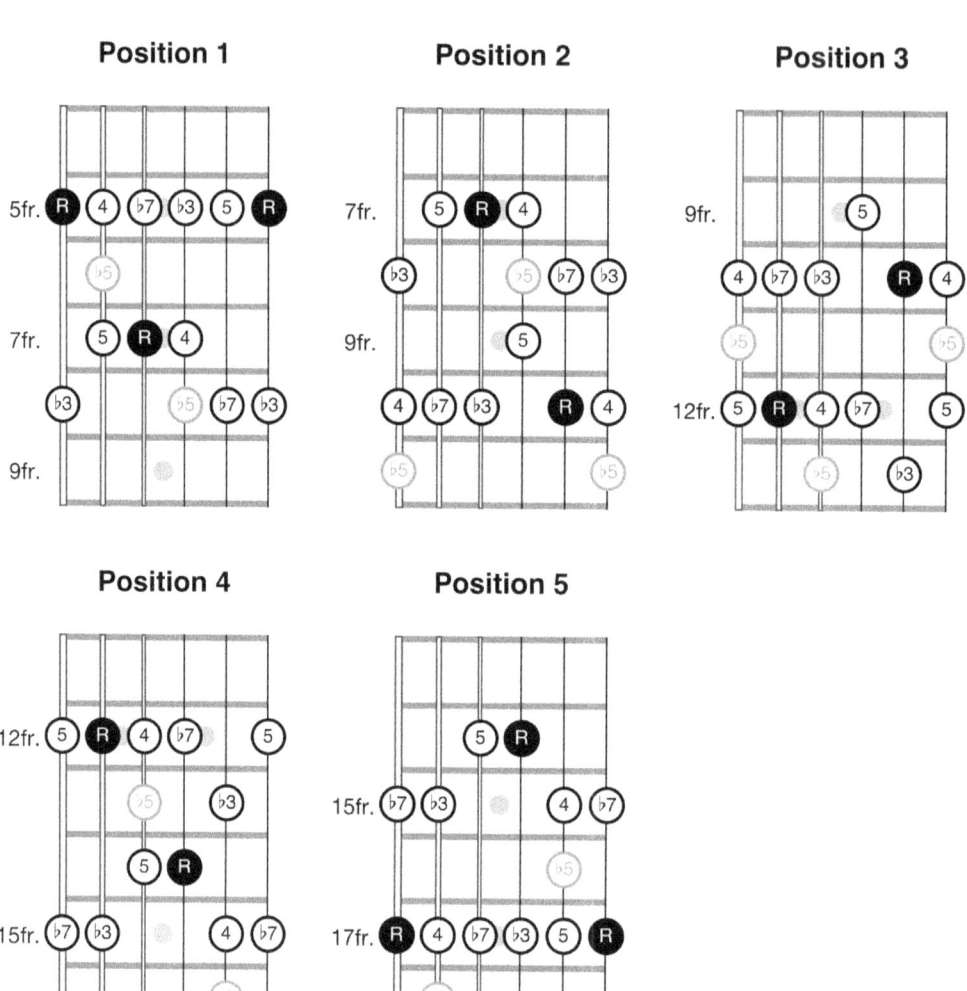

Exercise 3

Start at the 1st position of the major or minor pentatonic scale and loop through its *relative* positions on the fretboard.

Using a metronome, start at the 3rd fret and play up and back through the G major pentatonic scale at a comfortable tempo. Repeat this with each subsequent pentatonic position until you reach the root position again (one octave higher at the 15th fret). After playing once through all five positions, reverse this exercise to loop through each pattern until you arrive back at the 1st position on the 3rd fret.

Now, repeat this same exercise in the key of G minor. Again, start from the 3rd fret, but this time cycle through each position of the G minor pentatonic scale.

Tip: As with the modal exercises, try finishing each position by playing through the root notes in that pattern. Take careful note of how the modal patterns overlap each pentatonic scale by using the same octave shapes.

Exercise 4

Start at the 1st position of the major or minor pentatonic scale and loop through its *parallel* positions on the fretboard.

Using a metronome, start at the 5th fret and play up and back through the A major pentatonic scale. Continue by playing through each subsequent pentatonic shape in *parallel* (starting from the same fret). Once you have played all five shapes in parallel, reverse this exercise and loop back through each pattern until you arrive back at the A major pentatonic scale.

Extra Credit

- Experiment with playing **Exercise 3** using various keys. If you run out of room on the fretboard, just loop back to the equivalent position one octave lower (below your starting point).

- Repeat both **Exercise 3** and **Exercise 4**. This time try including additional notes from the major and minor blues scales.

5

Arpeggios

After looking at both modes and pentatonic scales, here we'll consider how arpeggios can be used to complement these core patterns.

Understanding Arpeggios

While arpeggios aren't traditionally categorized as *scales*, they're so regularly used in connection with scales (or even in place of them) that it makes sense to give them equal importance. Here's a brief overview of the arpeggios covered in this section:

Major Arpeggio

- **Type:** Major
- **Formula:** R - 3 - 5
- **Structure:** W+W - W+H
- **Description:** The major arpeggio is structured using notes from the basic major chord. It shares intervals common to all major modes and major pentatonic scales.

Minor Arpeggio

- **Type:** Minor
- **Formula:** R - ♭3 - 5
- **Structure:** W+H - W+W
- **Description:** The minor arpeggio is structured using notes from the basic minor chord. It shares intervals common to all minor modes and minor pentatonic scales.

Major Seventh Arpeggio

- **Type:** Major
- **Formula:** R - 3 - 5 - 7
- **Structure:** W+W - W+H - W+W
- **Description:** The major seventh arpeggio embellishes the sound of a major arpeggio, giving it a sweeter, more colorful tonality. It shares intervals common to both the Ionian and Lydian modes.

Minor Seventh Arpeggio

- **Type:** Minor
- **Formula:** R - ♭3 - 5 - ♭7
- **Structure:** W+H - W+W - W+H
- **Description:** The minor seventh arpeggio extends the sound of a minor arpeggio, giving it a richer sonic quality. It's essentially a minor pentatonic scale minus the 4th degree, and it shares intervals common to all minor modes.

Dominant Seventh Arpeggio

- **Type:** Major
- **Formula:** R - 3 - 5 - ♭7
- **Structure:** W+W - W+H - W+H
- **Description:** The dominant seventh arpeggio embellishes the sound of a major arpeggio, this time with a flattened 7th. Sounding less resolved and bluesier than a major seventh arpeggio, it shares intervals common to the Mixolydian mode.

Minor Seven Flat Five Arpeggio

- **Type:** Diminished
- **Formula:** R - ♭3 - ♭5 - ♭7
- **Structure:** W+H - W+H - W+W
- **Description:** Also known as the *half-diminished* arpeggio, this pattern is essentially a minor seventh arpeggio with a flattened 5th. It sounds extremely tense and dissonant and shares intervals common to the Locrian mode.

Using Arpeggios

Heavy use of arpeggios is often synonymous with styles such as classical or jazz. In reality, however, their usefulness far exceeds any one particular genre. In fact, in numerous situations you may find a strong understanding of arpeggios is equally, if not more important than a comprehensive knowledge of scales.

Like scales, arpeggios are a series of notes with fixed intervals. However, unlike scales, arpeggios are composed solely of chord tones. In using arpeggios, we're essentially interpreting chords as scales. Generally, the larger interval gaps we find in chords impart a greater sense of melodic flow into our phrasing. Beyond this, there are several other benefits to this approach.

First, arpeggios can function as a central melodic framework around which we structure our musical ideas. The notes in any scale have a different tonal character in relation to one another. Some sound tense and unresolved, while others sound strong and stable. Although this contrast is an important dynamic in music, *chord tones* are often the more desirable notes to emphasize in a melodic phrase. Centering around and embellishing arpeggio shapes relating to the tonic chord of a key is an extremely useful device for doing this.

> **Tip:** *This doesn't mean melodic ideas should only use chord tones. Additional notes are vital for adding color and interest to a melodic passage. It simply implies that chord tones are typically the stronger, more resolved-sounding notes.*

Many guitarists also use arpeggios to accent chord tones, not of an overall key, but of each individual chord in a progression. This technique is commonly referred to as *playing over the changes* or *chord-tone soloing*. Similar to the way pentatonic scales are sometimes used, a guitar player will structure their melodic ideas around the arpeggio shapes corresponding to each chord being played. This approach is used to reinforce the mood and momentum of a chord progression. The technique is extremely common in jazz but can also be found throughout numerous other genres.

Additionally, arpeggios can be used to navigate tricky or unexpected chord changes in a progression. For example, if a non-diatonic chord is introduced into a progression, rather than shifting temporarily to a different scale, it's often simpler to use an arpeggio pattern instead. In this way, playing notes from the corresponding arpeggio is useful for navigating potentially awkward changes with minimal fuss and without resorting to alternate scales.

Note: Like chords, arpeggios can be extended or altered. It's common to add chord *extensions* (e.g., 9, 11, or 13) or *alterations* (e.g., ♭5 or ♯5) to arpeggios for added color. This can be used to more accurately mirror the exact chord we're playing over.

Arpeggios can also be used to emphasize *sweet notes* and other interesting tonalities over either a particular chord or an entire progression. In this situation, we can imply the sound of one arpeggio where you might expect to hear another. For example, in the key of E minor, a Gmaj7 arpeggio can be built from the 3rd of an Em7 chord (using notes from the same scale). Rather than clashing, the two will sound harmonious together. This is because a Gmaj7 arpeggio uses notes from the Em7 chord and simply adds the 9th extension on top. While the concept of *superimposing* arpeggios sounds relatively advanced, a little experimentation with this idea can produce some very pleasing results.

Finally, arpeggios can sometimes be used in *parallel*. As with both pentatonic scales and modes, there are situations where you could use seemingly unrelated arpeggios from the same root note. Playing a minor seventh arpeggio over a major blues progression or using a minor seven flat five arpeggio in a minor blues solo are both examples of this. Again, careless use of this type of technique can produce haphazard results.

Summary

As with the other scales covered, the intention hasn't been to provide an exhaustive theoretical analysis. The goal has been to offer some context and explanation of how important these patterns can be for your creative vocabulary on guitar. We can summarize the popular uses for arpeggios as follows:

- **Used as Melodic Devices:** Arpeggios are often used in improvisation and composition for their flowing, chord-based melodic quality.

- **Used Over Chord Changes:** Along with additional melodic embellishments, arpeggios are commonly used to emphasize the chord changes in a progression.

- **Used Over Non-Diatonic Chords:** Arpeggios can be used as a simple way to navigate potentially awkward chord changes without resorting to additional scales.

- **Used in Substitution:** Different arpeggios sharing similar chord tones can be superimposed over a chord or progression to imply a richer harmonic character.

- **Used in Parallel:** Sometimes, seemingly unrelated arpeggios can be used in parallel to add tension or dissonance to a melodic sequence.

Tip: Unlike modes and pentatonic scales, the various arpeggio patterns in the following sections don't reuse the same core shapes. However, like modes and pentatonic scales, they're all based on one of the five octave shapes covered in **Chapter 2**. This means each shape will still share some core similarities.

Playing Arpeggios

Since arpeggios commonly comprise just three or four notes, there are numerous possibilities for playing them on the fretboard. While arpeggio patterns can be extended across all six strings, they're often broken down and used in numerous smaller variations. Despite this, all arpeggio shapes can be traced to one of five basic chord forms: C, A, G, E, and D. Like scales, each of these patterns also aligns with the fundamental octave shapes covered in **Chapter 2**. Below are two examples that demonstrate this using both the Amaj7 and Am7 arpeggio patterns based around an E barre chord shape.

Example 5.1

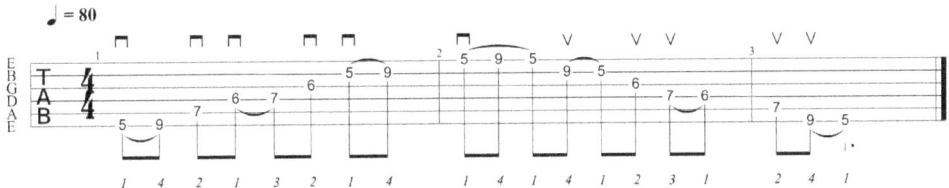

Example 5.2

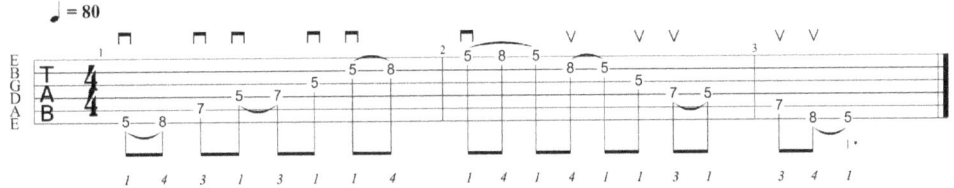

Finger Position

Unlike the scales we've looked at, the following arpeggio patterns will vary broadly when it comes to finger position. Depending on how they're played, arpeggios will often use one, two, and sometimes three notes per string. This will require some creative license as you work through each pattern. However, the previous examples highlight a couple things to keep in mind:

- First, sometimes the position each finger gravitates to naturally may not be the optimal choice for achieving smooth, flowing movements. In the first example, the half-step movement between notes on the 4th string uses the 1st and 3rd fingers. While the 1st and 2nd fingers might feel more natural, this would make it much harder to navigate the rest of the pattern. Try to think a note ahead of the one you're playing.

- Second, arpeggio patterns often use consecutive notes on adjacent frets. As seen between the 2nd and 3rd strings in the second example, this means multiple notes can be fretted by the same finger. This technique is similar to a small barre, except it requires a slight rolling motion so each note sounds cleanly without ringing into another.

Note: Each pattern outlined in the following sections is a highly useful recommendation. However, since there are many ways to play any arpeggio, experimentation with alternate patterns is also encouraged.

Picking Technique

Alternate picking could be applied to these patterns, but this isn't the suggested approach. Instead, *sweep* picking is a popular method that's often used when playing arpeggios. It's an extremely beneficial technique for cultivating fast, smooth movements. As seen in both examples, it requires that all ascending note sequences be downstrokes, and all descending note sequences be upstrokes. This differs from strumming, because all notes are still picked independently and aren't intended to ring into one another. For this to work, not every note can be picked. As shown, it will be necessary in places to make use of *hammer-ons* when ascending and *pull-offs* when descending.

Major Arpeggios

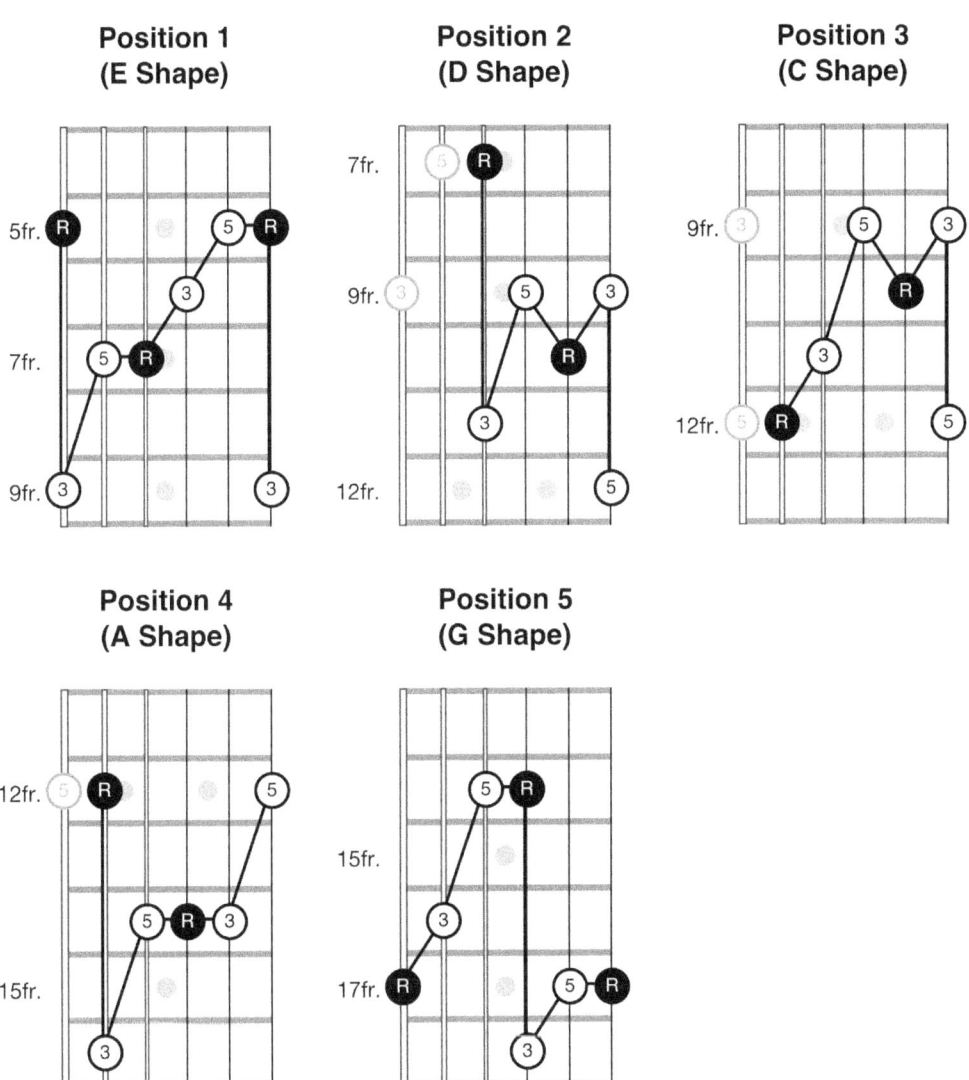

Note: Each pattern is referenced by its relative position to the other scales we've looked at and also by the basic chord type it represents. Since not all chords extend across all strings, the light gray notes show how each pattern can extend below the root note when needed.

Minor Arpeggios

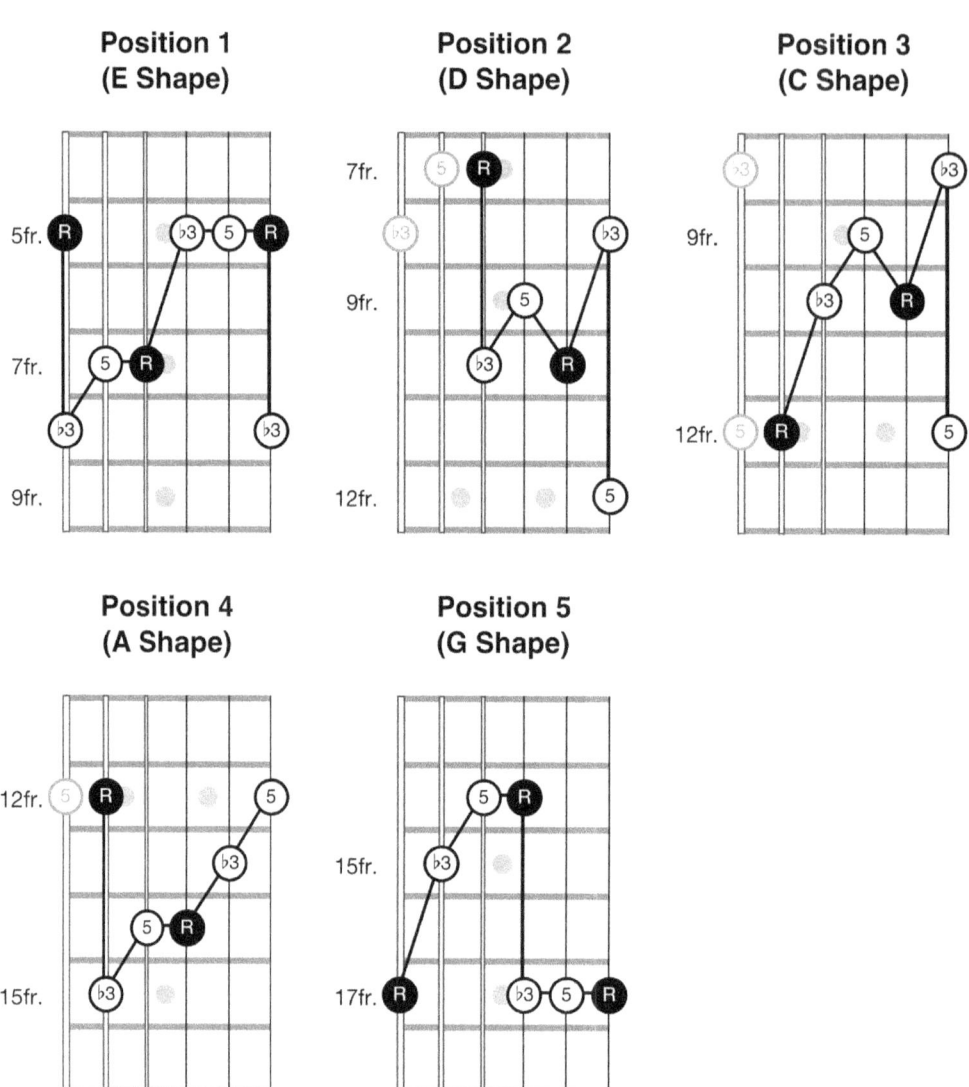

Major Seventh Arpeggios

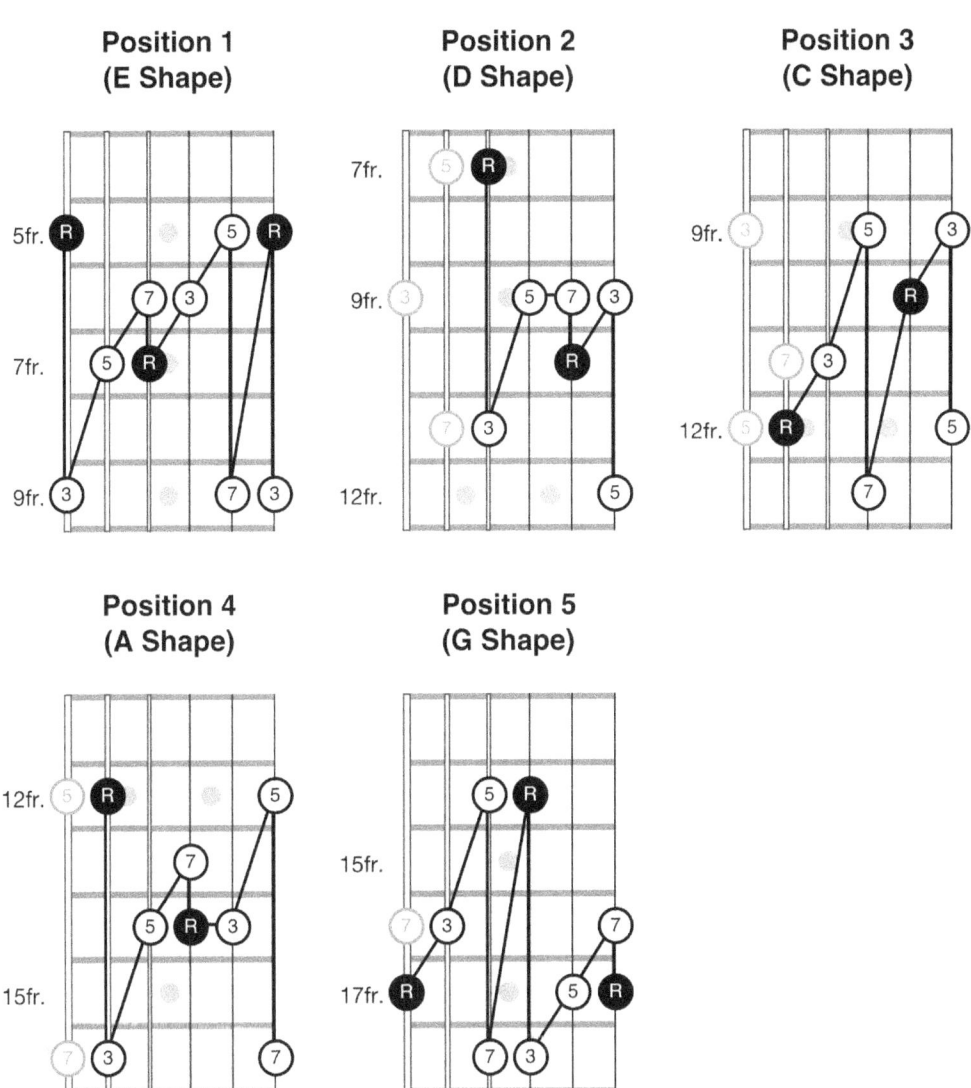

Minor Seventh Arpeggios

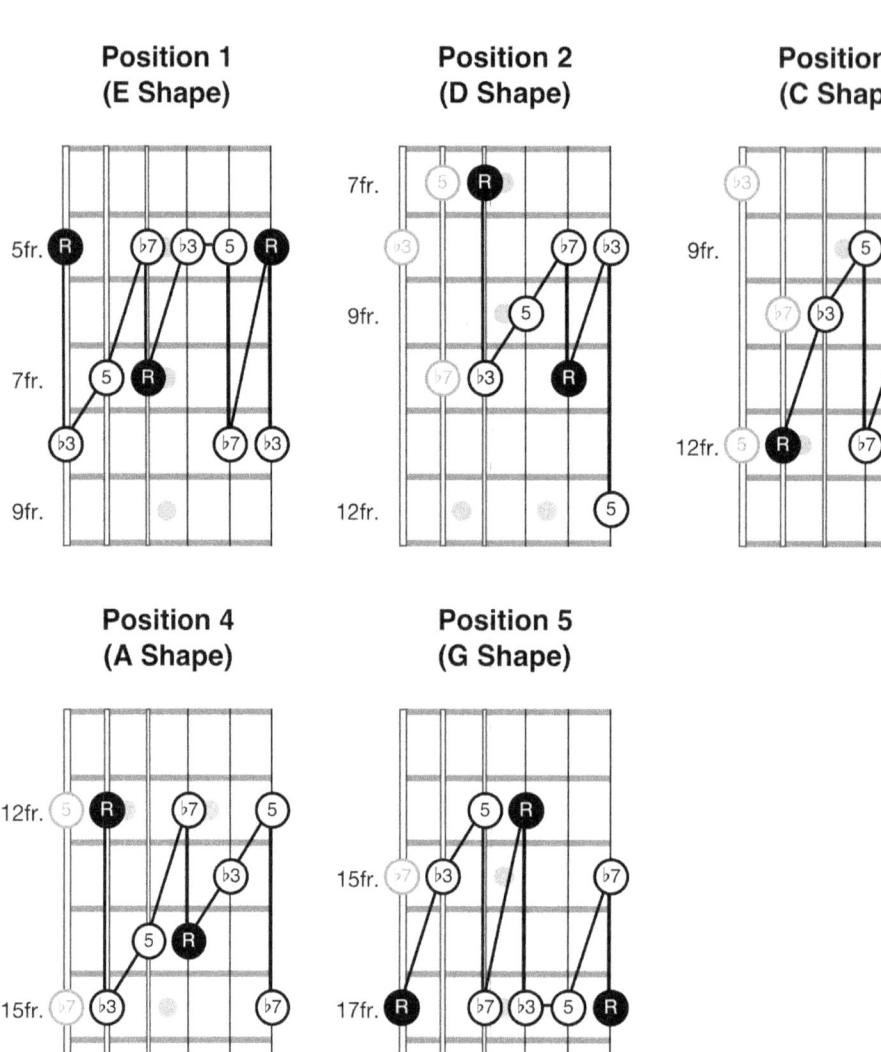

Dominant Seventh Arpeggios

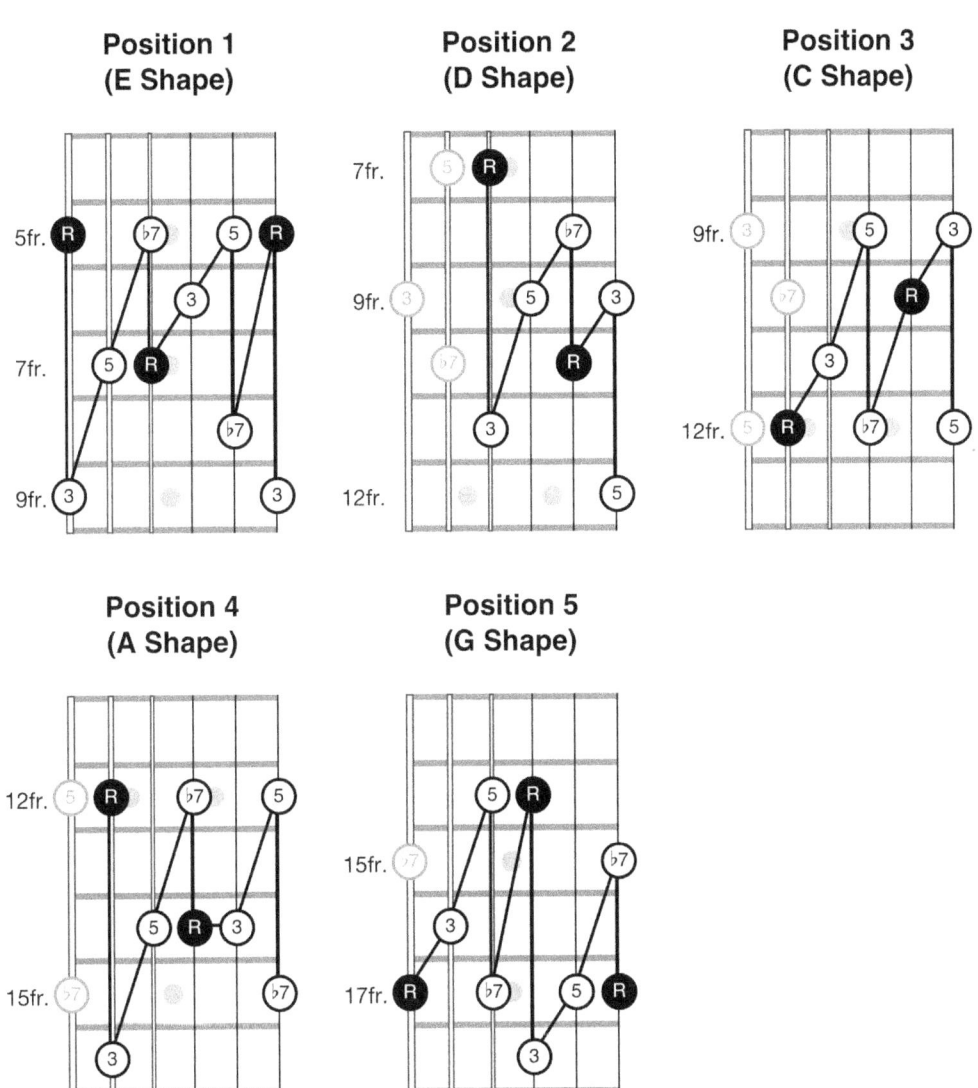

Minor Seven Flat Five Arpeggios

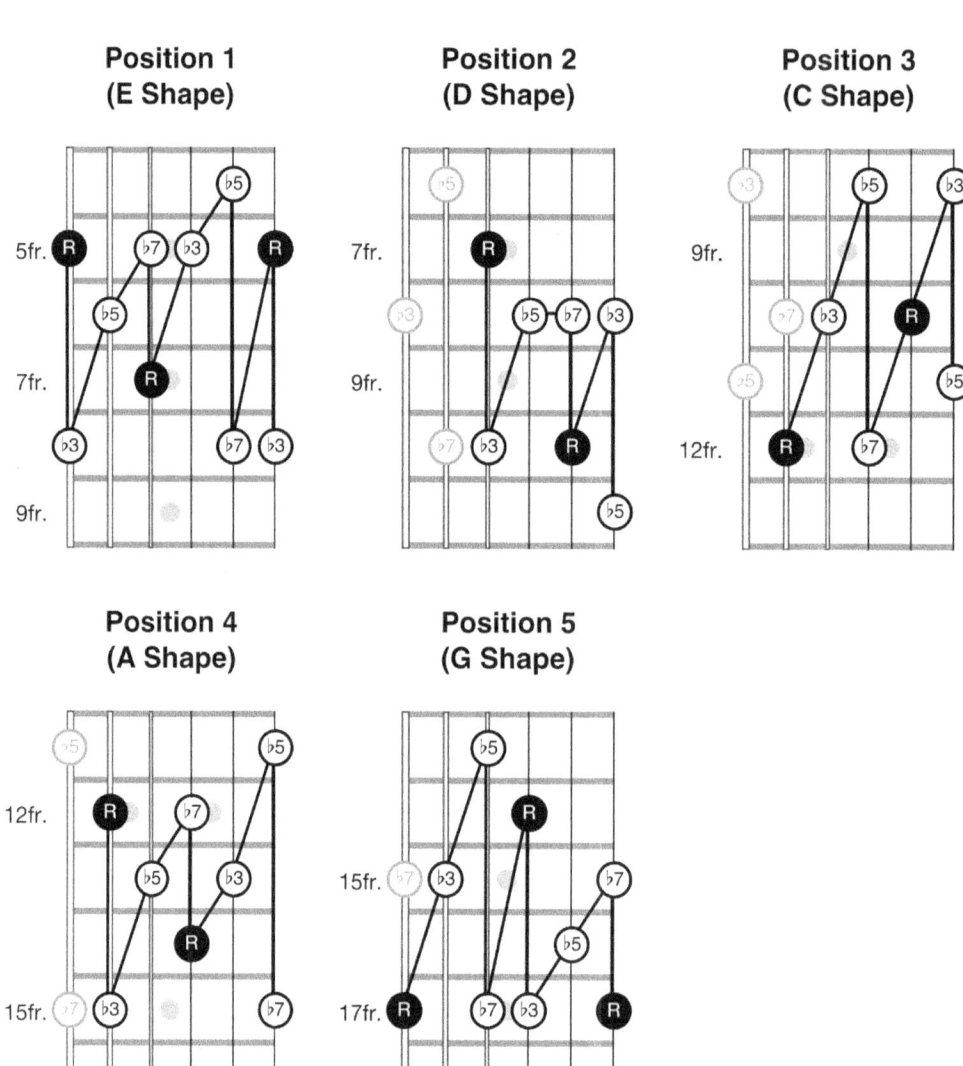

Exercise 5

Start at the E shape of the major or minor arpeggio and loop through its *relative* positions on the fretboard.

Using a metronome, start at the 3rd fret and play up and back through the G major arpeggio (E shape) at a comfortable tempo. Repeat this with each subsequent G major arpeggio (D, C, A, and G shapes) until you reach the E shape again (one octave higher at the 15th fret). After playing once through all five positions, reverse this exercise to loop through each pattern until you arrive back at the E shape on the 3rd fret.

Now, repeat this same exercise in the key of G minor. Again, start from the 3rd fret, but this time cycle through the various G minor arpeggio shapes in sequence.

Tip: As with the other scales, pay attention to the octave shapes within each pattern. This time, however, note the specific chord type (C, A, G, E, or D) that coincides with each unique octave shape. This will be the same for both major and minor arpeggios.

Exercise 6

Start at each position of the major seventh arpeggio and loop through the *parallel* seventh arpeggio patterns on the fretboard.

Using a metronome, start at the 5th fret and play up and back through the Amaj7 arpeggio (E shape). Continue by playing through each *parallel* variation of this seventh arpeggio, starting from the same root note (Am7, A7, and Am7♭5). Once all four shapes have been played in parallel, reverse this exercise and loop back through each pattern until you arrive back at the Amaj7 arpeggio.

Now, repeat this same exercise in each subsequent position of the Amaj7 arpeggio (using each D, C, A, and G shape variation). Again, start from the same root note and this time loop through each seventh arpeggio pattern in parallel.

Extra Credit

- Practice playing **Exercise 5** using not only major and minor arpeggios but all the seventh arpeggio variations as well.

- Experiment with playing **Exercise 6** starting from root notes on the fretboard other than A. Be sure to practice positions both above and below the 12th fret.

6

Scales in Context

Now that many essential concepts for using scales and arpeggios have been covered, let's conclude by looking at these patterns in context.

Thinking in Context

In the previous chapters, we've taken a detailed look at octave shapes, modes, pentatonic scales, and arpeggio patterns. We've also discussed essential concepts for learning scales, looked at popular uses for each pattern, and introduced some key practice exercises.

Admittedly, a significant amount of information has been covered. Since the intention has largely been to stay within the diatonic realm, however, you could say we've been looking at the same group of notes, just from different perspectives. In other words, there's an inherent connection between each pattern covered. Although it's important to learn each one separately, thinking of them merely as *isolated* shapes is significantly less helpful than viewing them in context with one another.

As stated earlier, the key to using these patterns together isn't to focus on their differences but on their similarities. While this will hopefully be apparent by now, below is a chart summarizing how these patterns are compatible with one another when improvising or songwriting.

Compatibility Guide

Modal Scale	Pentatonic Scale	Arpeggio Pattern
Ionian R - 2 - 3 - 4 - 5 - 6 - 7	Major/Major Blues R - 2 - (b3) - 3 - 5 - 6	Major/Major 7th R - 3 - 5 - (7)
Dorian R - 2 - b3 - 4 - 5 - 6 - b7	Minor/Minor Blues R - b3 - 4 - (b5) - 5 - b7	Minor/Minor 7th R - b3 - 5 - (b7)
Phrygian R - b2 - b3 - 4 - 5 - b6 - b7	Minor/Minor Blues R - b3 - 4 - (b5) - 5 - b7	Minor/Minor 7th R - b3 - 5 - (b7)
Lydian R - 2 - 3 - #4 - 5 - 6 - 7	Major/Major Blues R - 2 - (b3) - 3 - 5 - 6	Major/Major 7th R - 3 - 5 - (7)
Mixolydian R - 2 - 3 - 4 - 5 - 6 - b7	Major/Major Blues R - 2 - (b3) - 3 - 5 - 6	Major/Dominant 7th R - 3 - 5 - (b7)
Aeolian R - 2 - b3 - 4 - 5 - b6 - b7	Minor/Minor Blues R - b3 - 4 - (b5) - 5 - b7	Minor/Minor 7th R - b3 - 5 - (b7)
Locrian R - b2 - b3 - 4 - b5 - b6 - b7	Minor Blues (no 5th) R - b3 - 4 - b5 - b7	Diminished/Minor 7b5 R - b3 - b5 - (b7)

To reiterate, pentatonic scales are made up of notes common to each of their respective major or minor modes. Likewise, both pentatonic scales and modes share intervals common to the basic major and minor arpeggios. Additionally, each minor mode is compatible with all minor seventh arpeggios, with only two of the major modes being compatible with major seventh arpeggios. In contrast, the flattened 7th in the Mixolydian mode gives it a dominant seventh tonality.

Note: The Locrian mode is the odd one out. It isn't compatible with either major or minor pentatonic scales or their respective arpeggios. However, if we omit the natural 5th, the minor blues scale can be interchanged with the Locrian mode.

Playing in Context

In this guide, we've explored visualizing various pattern *types* along with numerous pattern *positions*. In total, this equates to almost 100 different positions on the fretboard, spread across 17 distinct scales and arpeggios. While this can seem intimidating, in reality working with this information is less complicated than it may appear.

As previously emphasized, not only is there a large amount of repetition between patterns, but each pattern can be reduced to one of five octave shapes (outlined in **Chapter 2**). To put this in perspective, below is a chart summarizing how each octave shape relates to the various positions of every pattern covered. Hopefully, now that you've worked through the previous chapters, these connections should be reasonably obvious. However, as a reference it's helpful to summarize how each position overlaps the others in context.

Navigation Guide

Octave Shape	Pentatonic Scale	Modal Scale	Arpeggio Pattern
Shape 1	Position 1	Positions 1 & 7	E Shape
Shape 2	Position 2	Position 2	D Shape
Shape 3	Position 3	Position 3	C Shape
Shape 4	Position 4	Positions 4 & 5	A Shape
Shape 5	Position 5	Position 6	G Shape

Note: While pentatonic scales and arpeggios fit neatly over the five octave shapes, modes will overlap the same reference point in a few positions. Also, each pattern in this chart is only categorized *generally*. This is because these respective positions will align, regardless of the specific pentatonic scale, mode, or arpeggio pattern used. (In all mode variations, the *relative* positions stay the same.)

> **Tip:** The emphasis here is how these patterns can be used interchangeably. This doesn't mean you need to use each pattern in every situation. It simply indicates that being aware of the way they're related on the fretboard provides more creative options for crafting melodic ideas.

Practicing in Context

As you become more familiar with each pattern, it's important to begin practicing them in context with one another. Until this point, each exercise in this book has centered around two key concepts: practicing in *relative* positions and practicing in *parallel* positions. Visualizing the relative positions of any scale pattern is central in fretboard navigation, allowing you to play over any key using any position on the guitar neck. Being able to visualize multiple parallel patterns within a single playing position is essential for playing over chord changes and seamlessly navigating through multiple keys.

While these are fundamental concepts for practicing scales, moving forward it's extremely beneficial to develop your own personalized playing routines. Ideally, you want to practice applying these patterns in real musical situations, not only by themselves, but also with one another. How you do this will depend largely on your preferred starting point for visualizing the fretboard.

If you're used to playing pentatonic scales, look at how the modal positions and arpeggio patterns overlap these core shapes you're already familiar with. If you favor the three-note-per-string framework, try incorporating different pentatonic and arpeggio licks into each modal position. If you like the chord-centered approach, focus on arpeggio patterns and practice embellishing them with notes from the surrounding pentatonic and modal scales.

Essentially, these are just different ways of working with the same information, but it's helpful to know which starting point seems the most logical to you. In general, a comprehensive practice routine might involve working through the mode, pentatonic scale, and arpeggio connected to each octave shape in all five positions on the fretboard. While the specifics of each pattern will change depending on the mode, the relative positions will stay the same.

> ***Tip:*** *Each mode will interact with pentatonic scales and arpeggios in a slightly different way. Initially, it may be helpful to focus on interchanging patterns using major and minor scales before working with the other modes.*

Ultimately, there are no *rules* for putting together your own practice routines. Other helpful practice habits might include practicing in different keys at various tempos, limiting yourself to specific areas on the fretboard, navigating through patterns using only two or three strings, or working with patterns linearly across a single string. Any exercise that helps you engage with these patterns from different perspectives is positive. Since musicality is always the goal, practicing in the context of songs and real playing situations will be of the most benefit.

Note: Want more help with this? Be sure to check out **5-Minute Guitar Jams** as a supplementary practice guide. This book features an album of high-quality backing tracks to accompany your practice.

Final Thoughts

Congratulations on completing **Learn Your Guitar Scales**!

If you've worked closely through each section, you'll now have a comprehensive framework for navigating the fretboard, crafting melodic ideas, and enhancing your improvisational skills. The intention hasn't been to overwhelm you with an encyclopedia of scale patterns (many of which you may never actually use). Instead, the goal has been to focus comprehensively on the core elements that are likely to form the bulk of your musical vocabulary on guitar.

This isn't to say a broader knowledge of scales won't be useful in certain situations, but simply that the greatest impact on your playing usually comes from understanding these central scale and arpeggio patterns. Beyond merely giving you shapes to memorize, the purpose has been to look at these patterns in context, discuss their common uses, and offer various tips and exercises for working practically with this information.

I sincerely hope this guide has helped answer questions, introduce new ideas, and lay solid foundations for ongoing study and experimentation. While a lot of ground has been covered, always remember: What we know is substantially less important than what we *do* with what we know. Learning scales isn't the same as making music, just as learning words isn't the same as talking. Both can open an entire world of creative potential, but neither makes sense unless they're being used to communicate or express something.

May this book help inspire you toward continued learning and creativity.

Liked This Book?

Did you find this book useful? You can make a big difference in helping us spread the word!

While it would be nice to have the promotional muscle of a major publishing house, independent authors rely heavily on the loyalty of their audience. Online reviews are one of the most powerful tools we have for getting attention and finding new readers.

If you found this book helpful, please consider helping us by leaving an online review at your place of purchase. Reviews needn't be long or in-depth; a star rating with a short comment is perfect. If you could take a minute to leave your feedback, it would be sincerely appreciated!

Additional Resources

For more resources, including great free content, be sure to visit us at:

www.guitariq.com

Stay in touch with all the latest news. To connect with us online, head to:

www.guitariq.com/connect

Would you like to read more? For a complete list of Luke's books, check out:

www.guitariq.com/books

Remember to grab your online bonus! Get the free bonus content for this book at:

www.guitariq.com/lygs-bonus

Interested in a master class with Luke? To check out his online workshops, go to:

www.guitariq.com/academy

About the Author

Having played for over 25 years, Luke Zecchin is an accomplished guitarist with a wealth of studio and live experience. Outside his work teaching music, Luke has toured extensively alongside renowned national and international acts, performing at everything from clubs, theaters, and festivals to various appearances on commercial radio and national television.

Playing lead guitar, Luke has worked on projects with established international producers and engineers. He has been fortunate to see these collaborations break into both the Top 50 ARIA Album and Singles charts, having also received nationwide airplay and notable debuts on the Australian iTunes Rock charts.

As the founder of **GuitarIQ.com**, Luke is dedicated to the education and coaching of guitar players all over the globe. With books available in over 100 countries worldwide, he has emerged as an international chart-topping author in his field.

Luke continues to work as an author and musician from his project studio based in the Adelaide Hills, South Australia.

Find him online at **LukeZecchin.com**.

www.ingramcontent.com/pod-product-compliance
Lightning Source LLC
Chambersburg PA
CBHW080414300426
44113CB00015B/2514